WHERE IS GOD IN ALL THIS?

LEONARD CHESHIRE

Where Is God
In All This?

interview by
ALENKA LAWRENCE

 St Paul Publications

St Paul Publications
Middlegreen, Slough SL3 6BT, United Kingdom

© St Paul Publications UK 1991

Cover design: Diane Edward
Cover illustration: © Robert Harding
Back cover photograph: Don Honeyman

ISBN 085439 380 3

Printed by Biddles Ltd, Guildford

St Paul Publications is an activity of the priests and brothers of
the Society of St Paul who proclaim the Gospel through the media
of social communication

Contents

Introduction   7

 1. Finding a faith   17

 2. War   39

 3. And peace   59

 4. Lessons of the disabled   81

 5. Family   103

 6. Suffering   121

 7. Prayer   145

 8. Travel   167

 9. Work   189

10. Journey's end   207

Introduction

It is easy to sum up a life as the stuff of legend; with Lord Leonard Cheshire, it's also true. How the young bomber pilot, celebrated war hero and witness to one of the twentieth century's most cataclysmic events, the dropping of the atomic bomb on Nagasaki, became the prayerful Catholic, charity worker and founder of Homes for the suffering and disabled all over the world, has never ceased to fascinate. In both stages of his career, he has remained the supreme individualist, never dodging controversy and inspiring and earning the respect and admiration of millions along the way. He has received two of Britain's highest honours: the Victoria Cross for bravery in war and the Order of Merit for his work with the disabled. Now in his seventies, he has embarked on a third, ambitious plan: his Memorial Fund for Disaster Relief.

Above all, Cheshire's thinking is governed by his strong religious convictions. And it is in that context

7

that he speaks frankly, in this series of informal interviews, about his life and work and the issues and events
that have moulded him: his wartime career and the
bombing offensive, his extraordinary conversion in the
unlikely setting of a London pub, the profound, and, he
believes, frequently misunderstood, effect on him of
his experience at Nagasaki, the care – and the contribution – of the disabled, the pressures of balancing work
and family life, his travels abroad and the special chal-
lenges he has faced in countries such as the USSR,
China, Japan and South Africa. Well-known for his
support of the nuclear deterrent as a means of prevent-
ing world war, Cheshire, speaking at the onset of the
Gulf Crisis, now looks to future peacekeeping and the
causes of conflict in the modern world. He reflects on
the commandment, 'Thou shalt not kill' in the context
of war, euthanasia and abortion. And he gives his
thoughts on themes of faith that have preoccupied him
through his own personal experience: prayer, suffering
and death.

His words, as I recorded them in the study of his
home in Cavendish, are spontaneous rather than pol-
ished. People may or may not agree with them; they
could be seen both as provocative and inspirational.
But even to those already familiar with his life story,
there will, I hope, be fresh insights into Cheshire's
thinking and his deep faith.

But first, a brief sketch of his life:

Leonard Cheshire, christened Geoffrey Leonard,
was born on 7 September 1917 – coincidentally in
Chester in the county of Cheshire, though he left it when

he was a year old. The son of a distinguished Professor of Law at Exeter College, Oxford, he had a happy and comfortable childhood, which included holidays at the Dorset cottage made famous by Thomas Hardy's novel *Tess of the d' Urbervilles*. He went to the Dragon School in Oxford and then won a scholarship to Stowe School in Buckinghamshire, where he was joined by his younger brother Christopher. The two boys, Leonard dark – and Christopher fair-haired, were very close, Leonard always very protective of his brother.

In 1936, Leonard Cheshire went to study law at Merton College, Oxford. At school, he had been a conscientious pupil, but at University things were somewhat different. His ambition, as he says himself, was for, 'a lot of money, a lot of excitement, minimum work and not to be a lawyer!' For a bet of a pint of beer he once travelled to Paris and back with only the 12/6* he had in his pocket, earning some more on the way by weeding a garden. He got his Law Degree, with Second Class Honours.

It was with the Oxford University Air Squadron that Cheshire learned to fly and he was commissioned as a Pilot Officer in the Royal Air Force Volunteer Reserve on 16 November 1937. A few weeks after war broke out in September 1939, he received a permanent commission in the Royal Air Force.

In June 1940, Cheshire joined his first operational unit, 102 Squadron, in Driffield, Yorkshire, and three nights later, the young Flying Officer Cheshire flew over Abbeville, in France, on the first of over a hundred bombing missions. In November, when piloting a Whitley bomber over Cologne, his aircraft was severely

* 62¹ᐟ²pence

damaged but he managed to complete his bombing run and bring the aircraft home. It earned him the first of three Distinguished Service Orders. A Distinguished Flying Cross was to follow.

Cheshire was determined to do his job thoroughly, even to the extent of blindfolding himself to learn to recognise the controls of his aircraft in the dark. His contemporaries talked about his fearlessness, his ability to inspire confidence, his fierce determination in pressing home an attack and – time and again – his care and humanity towards the men under his command. Once he took his entire ground crew for a celebration to a hotel bar reserved for officers – when a senior Army officer protested, Cheshire silenced him by saying, 'We work together. My life depends on them.'

By March 1943 the twenty-five-year-old Cheshire was the youngest Group Captain in the RAF, and in command of an RAF Station. But he longed to get away from his administrative job and back to operational flying, even though it meant dropping rank. Then, in September 1943, he was given command of one of the most famous of British Squadrons, 617, the 'Dambusters', which had been created especially to destroy the Ruhr dams with the so-called 'bouncing bomb'. It was a hard act for Cheshire to follow, but he soon made his own individual mark on the Squadron, personally leading every one of its raids during the next year. From the beginning, he was a strong advocate of low-level marking for more accurate bombing, a skill which became 617's speciality. It culminated in the destruction of Hitler's secret weapon, the V3, a huge gun capable of putting a shell into London every twenty minutes and kept under fifty foot of reinforced concrete which no ordinary bomb could pierce.

Cheshire was to become the RAF's most highly decorated wartime pilot. In September 1944 he was awarded the Victoria Cross, Britain's supreme military honour for bravery. Unusually, he did not receive it for a single act, but for four and a half years of sustained courage. He was told that there was to be no more operational flying for him but he could have any desk job he wanted. He chose to be posted to Calcutta, as it was furthest from the Air Ministry and he thought he might be able to get back to flying. There he was part of the tactical planning staff of Eastern Air Command, where the enemy was not Germany but Japan. Soon afterwards, he was sent to Washington DC as part of the British Joint Staff Mission.

Then, on a brief return visit to London in July 1945, a chance few words spoken in a London bar led Cheshire, nominally an Anglican, but with no religious faith to speak of, suddenly and dramatically to a staunch belief in God.

Another watershed in his life followed almost immediately. He was chosen by the Prime Minister, Winston Churchill, as the British observer to accompany the American mission which dropped the atomic bomb on Japan. He was to report back to the Prime Minister about the implications of the new weapon for future aerial warfare. With him in the B-29 observer aircraft which flew to Nagasaki went British scientist Dr William Penney, who had played a part in building the bomb.

Leonard Cheshire left the RAF after the war with a disability pension. The doctors said he was overworked and needed a rest. He tried various kinds of activity, including writing articles for the Sunday Graphic newspaper; in one, he proposed the idea of a

community scheme for ex-servicemen which would
attempt to regain something of the spirit of togetherness which had so impressed him in the war. He called
it 'VIP' (*Vade in Pacem*), bought a twenty-five bedroom house, Le Court, near Liss, Hampshire, from his
aunt with a hundred per cent mortgage and in the beginning the scheme had considerable support. But tired-
ness got the better of him again and his doctor told him
to go abroad for six months, which he spent in the
solitude of the Rockies in British Columbia, working as
a logger. When he returned to Britain, he found VIP
had collapsed. He was left with a ramshackle house and
eighteen and a half thousand pounds' worth of debts.
He had to sell virtually everything he had, from the
estate farm and thirty cottages, to his furniture. Then,
out of the blue, came a phone call from the Matron of
the local hospital. Arthur Dykes, VIP's pig-man, was
dying and had no relatives to look after him. Cheshire
took him in and nursed him single-handed until his
death on 22 August 1948, by which time another patient, an old lady, had joined them. More followed and
Le Court became a sanctuary for the sick and disabled
who had nowhere else to go. It was run on a shoestring
with residents paying only what they could manage,
and voluntary donations sometimes appearing just in
the nick of time. Meanwhile, Cheshire's new-found
religious faith led him to search for a Church that could
fulfil his expectations. In 1948, he became a Catholic.

Then, with his first Home at Le Court established
and a committee running it, he thought it was the end of
that period in his life. He took a job with Barnes Wallis,
inventor of the Dambusters' 'bouncing bomb', on a
new project for swing-wing aircraft which then moved
down to Preddanack in Cornwall. While he was there,

Cheshire got a letter from an epileptic boy whom Le Court wouldn't take. It eventually led to a second Home, St Teresa's, on the abandoned RAF station.

But he was getting more and more tired and kept going down with flu. In spite of that, he would preach with the Catholic Missionary Society, standing in the market places of Cornish towns. One day, a local priest said, 'I'm taking you off to hospital.' Vainly insisting that he had work to do, Cheshire was bundled into a car and, at the local hospital, diagnosed as having severe TB of one lung. A lot of his early patients had been terminal TB cases and he had had no proper means of dealing with their sputum. Not even allowed to go home to collect his things, Cheshire spent the next two and a half years until the winter of 1954 on his back in a sanatorium at Midhurst in Hampshire and had a series of major operations. He spent a lot of time studying theology and scripture but also started two further Homes from his bed.

While he was in the sanatorium, a Scotsman living in South India wrote to him and asked him to consider opening a Home there. In 1955 Cheshire arrived in India with just £100 in his pocket; two years later he had six Homes in there. There are now around 270 'Cheshire Homes' for disabled people from 18 years to 60 upwards in over forty countries, including the United States, Chile, South Africa, Papua New Guinea, the Philippines, Ethiopia, Thailand and Japan. Two significant recent ventures have been the opening of Homes in China and the Soviet Union. After meeting a sixteen-year-old paralysed boy in the early days at le Court, Cheshire identified a particular area of need and since then, his Homes have concentrated chiefly on the long-term physically disabled, particularly young adults.

In the late 1950s, Cheshire handed over their adminis-
tration to a body of Trustees but he still takes an active
role in initiating new projects and constantly visiting
the Homes, which are run by local committees responsible to the central Foundation in the country concerned, each country being legally autonomous but keeping to Cheshire's general principle that the disabled
residents must be involved in the decision-making of
their Homes.

At an early stage, the Foundation also took an
active interest in the mentally handicapped and now
has thirty Homes for them worldwide. More recently, it
has initiated family support services to enable disabled
people to live in their own homes. This movement is
now spreading to overseas countries.

In 1981, Cheshire's work for the disabled earned
him another top British accolade: he became a member
of the Order of Merit, which is limited to only twenty-
four living men and women at one time, chosen personally by the Queen.

In 1941, Cheshire, waiting to ferry a plane from
Canada, had visited America, where he met and married Constance Binney, a twice-divorced former film
star, eighteen years older than him. By the end of the
war the marriage was over.

After his conversion, he seriously considered becoming a monk and was greatly inspired by his first
visit, in 1949, to the Benedictine monastery at Solesmes
in Sarthe, west of Paris and later the Carthusians at
Parkminster in Sussex.

He decided, however, that his vocation lay with
his Homes and in 1959 he married fellow Catholic
convert Sue Ryder, who had also earned acclaim through
charity work, this time with displaced persons in Eu-

rope and the victims of the concentration camps. They have two children, Jeromy and Gigi. Leonard Cheshire, who was made a life peer last June, and his wife, who was given a life peerage with the title Baroness Ryder of Warsaw, in recognition of her work, live among the community of the sick and handicapped at the Sue Ryder Foundation Headquarters at Cavendish in Suffolk. They have a small flat in the part-sixteenth century house and brought up their children there. At the time of their marriage they hoped that their two foundations would merge but their supporters wouldn't accept it, so instead they founded the Ryder-Cheshire Mission for the Relief of Suffering, to undertake a few specialised projects outside the scope of their existing work. The first of these was the community of Raphael, at Dehra Dun in the foothills of the Himalayas in northern India.

Because he believed strongly that the force unleashed at Hiroshima and Nagasaki had made future war between the great powers inconceivable, Cheshire always remained a strong advocate of the nuclear deterrent as a means of keeping the peace. During the 1980s, he took part in a much-publicised series of debates with another prominent Catholic who held the opposite view, the then Monsignor Bruce Kent, General-Secretary of the Campaign for Nuclear Disarmament (CND).

Cheshire has become well known for his deep devotion to prayer and when asked his view about delicate issues, he frequently says, 'We should pray more.' At home in Cavendish, he has a chapel and also attends Mass frequently at the Augustinian Priory at nearby Clare. He goes for an annual retreat to his old mentors, the Carthusian monks at Parkminster.

On one wall of his study at Cavendish, Cheshire

has made an elaborate chart, like a child's classroom prop, showing the progress of evolution, which fascinates him. The chart exists alongside photographs from his wartime career and poignant images of the disabled people in his Homes.

And in his early 70s came a third phase in his life. In September 1989, the fiftieth anniversary of the outbreak of World War Two, he launched an ambitious global plan, the Memorial Fund for Disaster Relief, in which he aims, over six years, the duration of World War Two, to raise five pounds for every one of the 100 million people killed in the wars of this century and to use the money to help the victims of disasters worldwide. He has refused to spend any money from donations on promotion or advertising, but supporters of the Fund continue to come up with ingenious fund-raising projects, including a spectacular rock concert in Berlin and the sale of pens made out of scrapped Soviet and American missiles.

Leonard Cheshire divides his time between Cavendish and a small flat above his London office. He travels abroad frequently – on an overnight train en route to a Home for the handicapped in India, on Concorde to New York to promote his Memorial Fund with the United Nations Secretary-General. In the course of his work he has rubbed shoulders with politicians, priests, soldiers, hard-nosed businessmen, the disabled and dying, the mentally handicapped, burnt-out leprosy sufferers and Mother Teresa of Calcutta – and all have a role in his story.

1
Finding
a faith

'You were a very brash boy you know!'

Lord Ellworthy,
later Marshall of the RAF, to Cheshire

So, tell me what you were like as a young man. Is it true that you were brash?

I don't think I was brash in the sense of wanting to hurt other people. I see myself more as self-assertive, extremely sure of my own opinions – and a little boastful. I didn't listen to the advice of Father and Mother. I would argue with people who were specialists in their field and I liked creating a sensation. I bought a 1750 supercharged Alfa Romeo with money that I hadn't really got and I was determined to set the speed record from London to Oxford. Those were the days when Oxford students weren't allowed to have a car, so I had to hide it away in a garage. I got caught for speeding by the police, not in the Alfa but in a tiny little old Austin Seven. I found the newspaper clipping the other day – it said 'Undergraduate Astonished', because my defence was that the car wasn't capable of going above 30 miles an hour! What I used to like doing as a student was standing on the pavement, waiting for a car to come and then, at the very last moment, dashing across the road in front of it. I used to dare people and say, 'Come on, I'll take you on; I can get closer to that car than you can!' Until one day my heel was caught on the nearside wheel and it pulled my shoe off. The driver slammed his brakes on and got out – he was a big fellow – and said, 'I think I'm going to hit you!' But it had a certain sense because it was teaching me to judge closing distances and how to keep my nerve, wasn't it! I think I had a feeling somewhere in me that, one day, I was going to be somebody important and I used to talk as if it had already happened.

*So was your choosing the Air Force a natural pro-
gression from the brashness and the fast cars?*

When you're at Oxford, just as at Stowe, you're
expected to join one of the cadet corps,* and as I was
always looking for the spectacular, I thought, 'I'm not
going to be an infantryman, I'll go for the cavalry', but
because it was so rough and you had to run at the horse
and somersault backwards off it, and the Sergeant
shouted at you from start to finish, I decided it wasn't
for me. Anyway I'm slightly afraid of horses, so I then
went for the most sedentary thing I could find – an
aeroplane. I applied to the Air Squadron and, through
Sam Ellworthy, who was a friend of the family and
stationed at RAF Abingdon nearby, I was invited to a
cocktail party, where I met the Air Squadron's Chief
Instructor, Charlie Whitworth, and I niggled him by
boasting about how good I was going to be as a pilot.
And he got so angry at this that he said, 'Whatever
happens I'm going to take this young pup up and I'm
going to make him so sick that he'll never want to fly
again!' In fact I thoroughly enjoyed the whole thing. I
think I was sort of made to be in an aeroplane. Nothing
to my credit, but it was just like that.

*I find it rather hard to believe that you had no religious
faith at all when you were young – there must surely
have been something there. After all, weren't you brought
up as an Anglican?*

I didn't pray as a child and I didn't pray as a
student – though of course it really depends what you

* Military training for students

mean by faith. Yes, nominally I was brought up as an Anglican, but Father and Mother weren't really believers. When we were on holiday at Marnhull, we did walk across the fields to church most Sundays – but only because it was a social convention. There were moments I must have had some, albeit puerile, belief, because I remember as a child saying, 'God is everywhere is he? Well, where is he? Up in the corner of that room?' I went through a short period at Stowe when I was converted; the school chaplain persuaded me that I should take it seriously and I was convinced – for a month or two. But there is one other memory that I have, a very clear one and in a sense a very extraordinary one. On my first summer holiday at Oxford, I went hitch-hiking in Ireland and somebody asked me to go to church with them. It was a Catholic Church and it made a profound impression on me. I came out and said, 'There's something real here; this is different from any other church I have ever been into,' and the feeling lingered, lingered a long time. I didn't persevere with it at the time, but it remained in my memory.

Didn't you find that, during the war, when surely at times you must have been, to put it mildly, scared out of your wits, that you offered up some sort of prayers? A little prayer of thanks, perhaps, when your wheels touched the ground? Did you never wonder what would happen if you were killed?

No, it didn't enter my head. God was not a factor in my life at all – I wasn't against God, but if you don't see him as a reality, then you just don't pray. People who wish they could believe in God can pray because they're at least questioning the possibility of God, but I wasn't questioning it at all. It was irrelevant to me. There was no one to say thank you to or ask for help. Actually, I don't remember being scared out of my wits, but the kind of courage that was called on me in the war, when I would either be hit or get through, was completely different from the kind needed when faced with physical assault and torture which you know is going to go on and on. I just can't conceive how anybody puts up with that.

The only time I half lost control of myself was after the attack on Munich in 1944, which was perhaps the most difficult that I ever did. Certainly I've hardly ever flown through so much flak. I was in a Mosquito with my navigator, Pat Kelly, and having achieved what we had been sent to do, we got out of the defences at about 2000 feet, and I said, 'Pat, we've made it – give me a course for home.' I'd no sooner said that than we were suddenly caught in searchlights and heavy flak – the fatal mistake was that we'd both dropped our guard. And suddenly it was too much for us. Pat swore like a trooper. He did nothing but swear for about two minutes, every word imaginable. And I was trembling and sweating. We had been hit often enough before but it had never affected me in this way. It taught me never again to say 'We're home', until the wheels actually touched the ground. Maybe I did say some prayer or other, but no, I've no recollection at all.

I didn't wonder about getting killed; I just lived. I think I can say that, other than during my time off, when I liked to enjoy myself, all I thought about was doing my job. I'd fly every minute I could to keep my hand in. You see in World War Two, so much was at stake. It wasn't just survival. We had an inner urge that really drove us. A Norwegian, Kare Stenwig,* who was in the Squadron, put his finger on it. About ten years ago, we were having an evening together and I said, 'That was an extraordinary thing, to leave your country and cross the hostile North Sea to come and fight with us.' And he said, 'Yes, but we had a cold inner anger at the thought of what the Nazis were doing.' I would never have put it that way but once he'd said it, I knew that was it. There was something inside me that drove me. I've never before or never since lived my life with so much intensity as in those six years of war. That people could behave as Hitler was behaving was an affront to our human values and dignity, and so we felt that nothing mattered except stopping him. And he was so much more powerful than we were that we had to give our all or we had no hope of defeating him. Now you may find that strange; you may say 'With your work with the Homes you must have had more of a sense of urgency', but, though I can't explain it, I didn't. In war it's easier. It's sink or swim. And you know that if the enemy wins, you go down.

Then how did your attitude to religious belief change?

Rather dramatically. I don't know the exact date but it was the 8th or the 9th July 1945. My brother Christopher had been shot down on the way back from Berlin and was a Prisoner of War. I was stationed in Washington DC and got news that he was home. I discovered there was a conference at the Air Ministry in London and put up a paper saying it was essential I should be there – I didn't think the people in Washing-

* Later Chief of the Norwegian Air Staff

ton would know a great deal of what was happening in London and I did exaggerate! So I came back for about four days – I couldn't stay longer – and we used to go out in the evenings, celebrating. One of these evenings, about five or six of us were in a pub in Mayfair. For some reason or another the conversation turned to religion and I thought 'What's more inappropriate for an occasion like this than religion? So, to put a stop to the conversation, I said, 'God is an inner conscience that all of us have, that tells us individually what to do.' Then somebody, a girl, said, 'You're talking nonsense. God is a person and you know it.' And I absolutely can't explain it, but suddenly I did know it. I knew it with an absolute certainty. It was the last place I expected religion to come up. We were having a fairly boozy evening and she was drinking more than the rest of us. I certainly wouldn't have expected that kind of remark from her. She was one of the party, just somebody I'd met during those few days.

So there you were, a man who could actually use the words, 'It changed my life', with some truth. But what does a person in that position do? How do you start sorting things out in your mind? And how did your life alter?

I realised very quickly that night in the bar that something was going to have to change and in a major way. I recognised it called for a big decision and that I couldn't run away from it. And the first reaction I had was, 'Well, if that is true, then, number one, there will be limits in my personal life beyond which I can't go.'

You mean in your relationships with women?

Yes, I suppose that was the first thing. I think I'd describe myself as just another young man of that age. In most areas of my private life, I didn't see many restrictions. I mean I knew I mustn't commit a crime, but as for most of the rest, well, the only thing that mattered was, 'Don't get caught!' So I recognised that I was probably going to need time and effort and help to reorientate my life and adjust to different standards. It wasn't only that; I did also have the feeling that there might actually be things asked of me that I might not want to do – I can't easily put it into words – lead me into different paths and I asked myself if I was willing to walk them. I had to go away and decide what the answer was, so I sort of hid it and didn't let anybody know that I'd taken this on.

But how does one suddenly feel that God exists?

For a long time I believed it was an intellectual, reasoning process and that I had come to a logical, rational conclusion. But over the past ten or twelve years, I've come to think that it wasn't that at all. It was an inner encounter. In some mysterious way I'd encountered God. I mean he'd encountered me. And my certainty about it derived from the fact that I knew it had happened and therefore no reasoning or argument against it had any effect on me. If you were crossing a lonely moor at night on your own and met somebody on your way and your friends at your destination tried to persuade you there was no one there, it wouldn't make you change your view.

We still put too much emphasis on the intellect in our relationship with God. As the relationship deepens, you realise that it isn't an encounter of minds, but of the whole person. An intimate, personal relationship. We know from the teaching of the Church that you cannot know God with the mind but you can experience his activity both in history and in your own life and in a certain sense you're aware of his presence, even if it's totally beyond your grasp. But it was a long time before I worked that out and it's interesting that spiritual writers say that it may take you a number of years before you can properly interpret an experience, or you'll interpret it in different ways as you go along.

But you must have been receptive in some way. Had something in you built up to make it the right moment – your war experience for instance? A month, say, or a year before, would your reaction have been different? And you've been very negative about your character. Perhaps you're not being fair to yourself.

Well, I did make friends easily and a lot of people have said I had a pleasanter side. I'm not aware of that, but, for example, somebody mentioned that her mother remembered how she was staggering home with her shopping and I ran up from behind and offered to carry her bags. I know that, in the Air Force, I really cared about my men. It's the Air Force that changed me. It's there I think I ceased being brash. I couldn't afford to be. The Squadron wouldn't let me be. And I think the war must have had a much greater effect on me than I realise even now. Facing me with reality. Facing me with death, subconsciously at least. And at the time of my conversion, I'd already come to the conclusion that, having survived, I must find something to do that would help build a better world. I felt we'd launched out on a job to be done and I owed it to those who had not survived to go on working for a better peace. You couldn't go through a war in which 54 million people had already died – and if I show you my flying training course group photo, there's not more than three that have survived – without realising that the end of the war wasn't the end of the job. So I was already in that general frame of mind, but I was still looking for a happy, excitable life. I wanted to be free to do what I wanted. I didn't want any rules to govern me.

So how did you come out of 'hiding' as you put it, and start, as it were, living your faith and sharing your experiences?

Obviously the answer to my encounter in the pub could only be yes, so my answer was yes. The next thing was, I realised I must find the Church. But I had to go back to Washington a couple of days later, so I asked somebody for a book and they gave me *The Screwtape Letters* by C.S. Lewis. In fact it was a rather good introduction to the Faith. It's very compelling isn't it? There was Satan as a person, and, reading through the Screwtape Letters, I could see myself in it and many of the sort of things that I went through.

And I can't think it was just a matter of chance that my encounter with God happened only a few days before I was sent for by Field Marshal Sir Henry Maitland Wilson, Chief of the British Joint Staff Mission, who told me that an atomic bomb had been built and that I was to be the British observer.

That was the first time I began to pray, but it was very rudimentary. I remember that, before the attack went off, a Protestant padre blessed the mission. The Americans find it quite easy to invoke God's blessing in their public affairs, but I wasn't used to it – the RAF didn't do it – and I felt it was slightly incongruous. Another thing I thought was, 'Is this compatible with what we're going to do?' Those who oppose the atomic bomb are just looking at a bomb being dropped on a city; they aren't looking at it in its whole context. But I can understand it, because I think I felt similarly at that moment. Suddenly confronted with the prayers, I was relating them to the dropping of the bomb on people and not to the reason why it had to be. For the first time, it made me think, 'How do I reconcile this with believing in a God who's a God of love?' I hadn't had the chance to address that question. But then I said to myself, 'Well, if we do what we believe is right then we have the right to ask God to watch over it.'

This will also tell you something of what I mean when I say I was a little full of self-importance when I was young. Maitland Wilson told me, 'You will now go to the Pentagon where you will get a more precise technical briefing. You are sworn to secrecy.' It was intimated that I would be followed. And I was to report back to Churchill on the implications of this bomb for the future of air warfare. Now that's quite a big brief! I'm not a natural keeper of secrets; I tend to want to talk about things. I had never thought I would ever meet a Prime Minister on official business. I didn't live in that sort of world. So you can imagine how it was going to my head; I began to picture myself seeing the Prime Minister privately, and him asking me to stand up in the House of Commons and make one of the most dramatic speeches ever made. I was trying to keep myself under control: 'Come on, pull yourself together, you're just a Group Captain and you're about ordinary business. You're lucky, you've come through the war alive; oth-

ers haven't. Just stop these stupid ideas.' But you know
how we human beings are. So you can see there was a
lot to grapple with: I had to come to terms with my
faith, the faith that I'd been given, and somehow I had
to come to terms with the nuclear age. All the way out
to join the atomic mission, I was wrestling with these
thoughts, I was being knocked about from side to side.
And for the first time, God was real, he was there. What
did that mean for me? How was I going to find out?

I can only say that it was a totally bewildering
time and in a way it was symbolised by the fact that we
were flying off into unknown territory. I'd never been
to the Pacific before. Our first stop was Honolulu and I
thought, 'Goodness, I'll see Waikiki Beach!' As a boy,
I'd heard about Waikiki Beach and seen it in films and
it meant paradise. But, when I got there, it was the
biggest disappointment I think I can ever remember!
The tide was in, the beach wasn't any wider than this
room, it was surrounded by great buildings, it just
looked completely ordinary. Then we moved off to
Kwajalein, which had been pulled out of the sea, a
coral reef, just big enough to build a landing strip.
Everything was completely new to me and in every
sense of the word, at every level of my being, we were
going off into the unknown.

*Once the atomic mission was over – and obviously I
want to talk about your feelings about that in greater
detail in a moment – what was it like coming down to
earth, as it were, after the excitement of the War? You
must have had difficulties readjusting.*

Yes, I've never been through two such turbulent
years. I didn't know where I was going. Trying to

adjust from war to peacetime life was quite a shock in itself. We'd had such a sense of common purpose in the war and suddenly it was gone, suddenly each man seemed to be looking for his own career – well he had to be. People who had safe jobs in the war emerged with the best positions; a lot of those who had fought in the front line came back to nothing. Things were turning upside down. Then I had new standards to build into myself – how difficult that was. I found that I couldn't bear to be alone. If I was invited out to a cocktail party, I would stay on right to the bitter end until everybody else had gone, hoping that my host would invite me on.

I just felt that I had got to do something that was helping build a better world – though that isn't how I would have put it then. The question was how. How on earth does an ordinary individual with no public position and no qualifications participate in the struggle to build a better world? I went from person to person; I followed path after path – some broad avenues, some tiny, murky alleyways. None of them led anywhere. I went through a little period when I thought about reincarnation – you know, you find something and think, 'This is it!' and then you find it isn't. My health wasn't good. I was having to come to terms with the fact that the war had taken more out of me than I realised. The Air Force put me briefly in a rehabilitation unit. I think it was a psychiatric rehabilitation unit; anyway, I just didn't like what was there, so I got out. Originally, I was looking for some great, world-beating crusade, some way of altering the way the world works. Obviously I couldn't find it.

So then on impulse I said, 'Forget your ideas. Do something.' And I launched out on a kind of community scheme aimed at helping ex-servicemen resettle into civilian life and at the same time trying to recapture something of the spirit of togetherness and sense of purpose of the war. It started with a bang and got a substantial public response and quite a lot of money. We lived in a commune, each person doing the work they could. One woman ran kennels, a blacksmith did wrought iron work to be sold, we had quite a bit of farming land, and the idea was that everybody put their profits into the common kitty and took out five pounds each a week. But things just didn't work – everyone blamed everyone else. Working with somebody else providing the money, you haven't the same responsibility as when it's your money. So the thing finally collapsed because it wasn't realistic.

And at the same time, how did you set about doing what you'd said you had to do, which was to find the Church? What made you choose the Catholic Church when you'd nominally been an Anglican?

Very soon I told myself that the Church should have two characteristics. The first was, it must speak with authority. I came across this early on when reading the New Testament. Remember the crowd's remark that Jesus was a man who spoke with authority, not like the Scribes? Now that is such a forceful statement, that I said to myself, 'Well in that case, if he founded a Church, then that Church must speak with the same authority as he did, and with the same complete certainty about what it's saying.' When I wanted to be a pilot, I would not have gone for instruction to someone who wasn't quite sure about whether the aircraft stalled at a given speed. I needed someone who knew what

they were talking about. And the second thing is, the
Church must claim the power to forgive sin, as Jesus
did.

Also, unless the Church was teaching us about
reality, it had no appeal for me. If it was merely offering some nice advice about how to lead a good life,
well that was something good, but it was not enough. I
wanted to know what the meaning of life was, what
happens after our life and what means we have to
employ to fulfil destiny. Who was God? What did he
want of us? Therefore when you look at the different
religions – and they've all got good in them, there's no
question about that – I think the important thing is to
ask, 'Is there one which God founded and God guaran-
tees?' If that wasn't the case, you could choose which
you liked. But if it is true, then clearly we have a duty to
look for it and, once we find it, to submit to it.

At first I thought finding the Church would be
simple, but having those convictions about authority
and the power to forgive sin meant that, in each section
of the Anglican Church I went to, I didn't find what I
was looking for. I found goodness and I found a lot of
very edifying teaching, but it wasn't right for me. The
Anglican Low Church* gives you a good deal of flex-
ibility. Evidently, in some sections of it, you don't need
to believe in the Resurrection. Only when I came to the
High Church did I meet authority, and I can't explain it,
but it didn't seem to ring true. I couldn't fault it ration-
ally, but it didn't feel like a natural authority, given
from above. To some people clearly it is – I'm not
trying to hold that one is better than the other. As I said
at the beginning, finding a faith was far more a recogni-

* The less ritualistic and sacramental wing of the Anglican Church

tion than a rational process. You instinctively feel authority. And this may sound strange, but when I see a clergyman I instinctively know whether he's a Catholic or not. And I respect priests greatly as God's representatives on earth. I've never felt happy calling them by their Christian names, and never do. So I think that, when Jesus says, 'My sheep recognise my voice' (Jn 10:14), there's something very profound there.

But being such an individualist, why did you feel you needed a Church at all?

Because faith in God is not enough until you become a member of the Church. Until then, you can't know Jesus is the gate and the road to God. So you have to hold as a Catholic – and I hold it totally – that your response to God can only be fulfilled adequately when you're within the Church, absorbing the teaching of the Church and participating in the Sacraments. So finding the faith in terms of knowing that God existed was the first thing; knowing that the Catholic Church was the true Church, and a few months later, becoming a member of it, was the second. That also happened rather dramatically and suddenly. The hospital rang and said Arthur Dykes, who had looked after the pigs on the community scheme, was dying of cancer. The hospital Matron told me, 'We can't keep him because he doesn't need treatment, just bed care and we've got a lot of people who could be treated waiting for his bed, so it'll have to be vacated. You're the man quoted as his sponsor, so will you please find somewhere for him to go?' I could find nowhere at all that would take him, so I took him to live with me.

Arthur was a lapsed Catholic – an Irishman – and

from that moment, he began to regain his faith. He asked for the Catholic priest, so I got Father Henry Clarke from Petersfield and I soon became quite friendly with him. Arthur impressed me deeply, because I was very enthusiastic and would ask quite profound questions about the faith and he would answer very simply in a way I could understand.

The Anglican clergy whom I met were also extremely friendly. They'd come and spend a couple of days with me and I'd go and stay with them. We'd have deep discussions, but they gave quite long answers which I didn't always understand. But if I were to ask Arthur for instance, 'How do you explain suffering?' he would give me an answer such as, 'the explanation is in the Cross'. Now that's not to say that I followed it, but it's the kind of simple answer that went straight to the heart, yet was different in kind from the reflective theological answers that the others were giving. I asked him, 'What is the purpose of life?' and he said, 'To love and serve God in this world and in the next to live with him in his very own home, Len'. He said it in a most appealing, simple but convincing way. He couldn't be clever, it wasn't his nature. He probably came from a farming background in Ireland. And it came from his heart; it wasn't just something he'd read – though I can now see that it was based on the Catechism – but it just carried a certain conviction. So did the way he talked about the Mass: 'Ah, the peace after hearing Mass,' he said more than once. I think it was as much the way he said it as what he actually said. If you didn't believe it, you understood it. He had a great sense of humour. I remember coming in one night and finding him eating a tube of toothpaste – he said he had indigestion, and he found toothpaste was the best cure! I remember washing his feet, because he couldn't wash himself and him saying, 'Very humbling, isn't it, Leonard.'

When Fr Clarke gave him the Last Rites I remember saying, 'Father, may I stay?' and he said, 'Don't be stupid, of course you can.' Arthur died around midnight and I had three hours to sit quietly with him. To while the time away, I picked up a book. It was Mgr Vernon Johnson's *One Lord One Faith* – he was a famous, very distinguished Anglican preacher who'd become a Catholic, which caused quite a stir. The book explained why, and as I read it, I said, 'This is what I'm looking for.' It was the first time I'd heard the Catholic Church say what she had to say for herself. I'd only heard what other people had said. It was exactly the same kind of certainty that I'd felt that night in the pub. Incidentally, I've been a bit remiss – I used to say publicly that the book was Arthur's but then someone wrote to me rather indignantly and said, 'I'm the man who led you into this!' I can't picture him. He was just a casual visitor. He saw I was searching and probably deliberately left the book there. It couldn't have been there by accident. I think in fact he's one of those people in one's life who does you a very good turn, but gets no credit for it.

So in the morning when I'd done the formalities, I said to Fr Clarke, 'I want to become a Catholic'. Our conversation went something like this:

'Nonsense,'

'Father, I do,'

'You didn't yesterday. It's completely irresponsible to make up your mind that quickly. I'm having nothing to do with it.'

'I'm very sorry, Father, but I mean it.'

'Why?'

So I told him about the book and he said, 'Well,

the Church of England has written an answer to that book. I'll get it for you and you read it. And if you're still of the same mind, come to me again and I'll think it over. Otherwise come to me in six months' time.' So I read the book, *One God and Father of Us All*, in good faith and it didn't alter my conclusion. The arguments may have been strong but to me they were off target. So I went back to him and in the end he agreed.

It used to puzzle me a bit. I was so totally certain that that first book I read answered my question, while the other, though very good and logical in its counter-arguments, didn't touch me. I think one answer I kept giving to people was that everything fitted. It was exactly like having a jigsaw puzzle in which every single piece was in place. And that was the most compelling, reasonable argument to me.

Very early on, Fr Clarke taught me how to find my way around the Latin Breviary* – it's quite complicated and I just couldn't remember enough of my school Latin to understand it fully, but I got the gist of it, so from that time on I learned to say the Office. I couldn't go to Mass every day because, before long, I had eight patients at Le Court and I was the only one to look after them. I couldn't disappear every morning for an hour and a half, so it was agreed I'd go twice a week.

That's more than a lot of people do! You sound as if you were rather going what some people would irreverently call 'over the top'. And weren't you just a little self-righteous?

* The Divine Office (Liturgy of the Hours). It is the public prayer of the Church comprised of hymns, Psalms, Biblical and spiritual readings, and prayers, sung or recited by the clergy, religious and by certain members of the Church, to sanctify the day and the hours.

Of course when you suddenly get the faith you're a bit over-enthusiastic. I suppose I'm impulsive by nature and I've got to put everything I've got into everything I'm doing, whether it's good or bad, and once I saw the Catholic Church as the true Church, the true faith, I was completely swept off my feet. I thought: 'This is something I must give my whole life to without reserve. So I took it to extremes. You don't carry it naturally and easily to begin with, you know, you're too self-conscious, so you're a bore to other people. I thought every Catholic must be a saint – that it would be impossible to have this marvellous Church founded by God with Jesus at the head of it guiding you and not be a saint, so when I discovered that some of them were far from it, it came as a real shock! I used to say the Office every day, I used to say three Rosaries.* I'd sit right into the early hours of the morning to say them. I wouldn't let them go. I thought it was a good thing to fast a lot. And finally Bishop Grimshaw of Plymouth, whom I had got to know quite well and with whom I used to stay at the Cathedral – I was down in Cornwall at the time – was horrified when I told him what I was doing and told me to stop! Fr Clarke was also a convert but he didn't really like what I was doing or think it was quite right. So I had a little battle with him, though we were very friendly and close.

Yes, perhaps I was a little self-righteous at first. But Fr Clarke had told me not to throw my past over-

* A devotional prayer consisting of the recitation of one 'Our Father, ten Hail Mary's, and a Glory be to the Father' for each of the fifteen decades, dedicated to fifteen Scriptural Mysteries of the life of Christ and his mother, Mary, as the topic of mental prayer; separated into three sets of five Mysteries – joyful, sorrowful and glorious – the Rosary focuses on the Incarnation, the sufferings, and the glorification of Jesus.

board, not to overlook the good that was in it and not to forget to be thankful for it. He encouraged me to go to Confession once a week and wouldn't let me get self-satisfied. There was no merit in me, there was merit in the faith, and when you look at the faith and think how poorly you're measuring up to it, I don't think you could be self-satisfied. I may have been over-confident when I was asserting the faith, but then I was asserting something I knew to be true. But I don't think I was attributing any of that to myself – at least I hope not.

2
War

'In four years of fighting against the bitterest opposition, he has maintained a record of outstanding personal achievement, placing himself invariably in the forefront of the battle. What he did in the Munich operation was typical of the careful planning, brilliant execution and contempt for danger which has established Wing Commander Cheshire a reputation second to none in Bomber Command.'

Cheshire's VC citation, September 1944

During the war, as you said, you didn't have the belief in God that you have now. But do you see those six years that you spent 'doing your job' as you put it - as part of your development as a Christian? Or as an aberration you could have done without?

You have to hold that, from the moment you're born, if not before you're born, God has a plan for you. He isn't helping you develop merely from the moment you become a Christian or have a faith. I have no illusions that it wasn't any effort of mine that brought me through, so it's clear to me what a debt of gratitude I owe. Why me rather than so many others, I can't begin to imagine. So, since I think I went through all that with no faith, no knowledge that God existed or the part he plays and all that he holds in promise for the future, receiving the faith means that much more to me. I paid no attention to God, did not try to pray to him, or thank him or anything, but still came through and not only came through but was greatly strengthened by the War.

That would appear to be a controversial statement in view of the terrible nature of war. How do you mean that you were 'strengthened'?

I think I was very blessed in the fact that the war came when it did, when I'd just finished university but hadn't yet committed myself to a job. The war taught me a lot of things – though I'm not saying I learned all the lessons. It taught me how to handle people; you've got to know how to communicate your objectives to the men under you, to be willing to take a reprimand and not take it personally, and you've got to be ready to tell people when they are wrong or when they are right. In

the Armed Forces it's easy, because you've got everything structured – you know exactly what you can say
and the other man knows his rights of comeback. In the
open market, where the moral law is looked on by
people as being restrictive, it's a bit different. I think
life in the Armed Forces taught me to search out and
know my objectives and priorities and to subordinate
the less important to the more important. I used to
spend hours teaching myself to fly completely relaxed
until there was no effort in it, so when it came to the
target, I could mobilise my full forces and I hadn't
expended some of them on the job of getting there.

The war gave me discipline, a sense of purpose. If
you think of the promise our faith gives us, you really
ought to let absolutely nothing stand in the way; everything that doesn't take you to your goal or give you
strength and encouragement to get there, when you
come to think of it, is a waste of time. Blindfolding
yourself and spending a long time walking round the
cockpit by some standards might seem a bit exaggerated, but if you take into account that you may be
coming back one night shot up with no lights on, and
survival may hinge on your knowing exactly where to
find the right switch, it's just a perfectly normal thing to
do. I thought I knew enough about the aircraft when I
arrived on the Squadron, but my Captain was a pre-war
pilot and he sat me down and questioned me and I
began to realise how little I knew. It wasn't just the
aircraft, it was knowing the target, the tactics and the
things you had to look out for. On my first trip, we only
had to bomb the bridge at Abbeville behind Dunkirk.
He knew what was going on, but everything was so
new and strange to me that I only had a confused,
limited picture of it.

Half a dozen trips later, I'd taken it in. I think the supreme example of this was when I came over Munich in 1944. The first difficulty was that the extra wing tanks which we should have had to get us there and back with a safety margin never arrived. But I'd been given the Mosquitoes* in answer to my plea for them, on condition that we marked Munich successfully and the main force detailed to bomb our markers did a good job. If I failed, then the Mosquitoes would be taken away. I risked not having enough fuel to get there and back safely, but I knew that, if I aborted the attack, I might not get another chance. There were four Mosquitoes and the crews of the other three didn't know the urgency; they thought I was taking an irresponsible decision. Anyhow, we arrived over the top of the target, but I could only identify it and mark it under the light of parachute flares and as I got over the target, these flares suddenly ignited. It was good timing, but ideally I should have been about a minute's flying time away so that I could identify my position, work out from there where the aiming point was and then be in the correct position to take a dive at it. In fact, as they ignited, I looked down and in a split second I saw my aiming point immediately beneath us – because I'd had to memorise the map and the photograph of the target area. In those days I was young and fairly well co-ordinated and had it well-memorised. I only had to take one look and I knew.

Now the problem was that, to do a proper run-in, I'd have to fly away, get into position and come back in, but I knew that if I did that I risked losing it or

---

* De Havilland (DH-98) Mosquito, British twin-engine, two-seat, mid-wing bomber aircraft.

maybe the flares might go out. On the other hand, if I went straight in from where I was overhead, that meant a vertical dive, and the two problems for that were, first that I'd exceed the safety-limit speed of the aircraft and nobody was quite certain what would happen if I did that, and secondly that if I released my markers in a vertical dive they would drop through the forward bulk-head, so first the aircraft would disintegrate and second I wouldn't hit the aiming point. And the only way around that was, as you released, to pull the stick gently back so that you lift the nose but not so hard that you throw the marker-bomb. I just knew I had to go, so I turned over on my wing-tip and pushed the nose and went straight down. I didn't look at the speedometer as I was committed to it. I could see the aiming point – the Gestapo Head-quarters – and held it right in my sights and when I thought I'd got about as low as I dared because I was building up speed all the time, I dropped the markers and pulled the stick back slightly. OK they didn't hit the forward bulkhead. I pulled up, but then of course there were lights above me and lights below me and shells bursting above me and so it was a very confusing situation. I didn't really know if I was upside down or what I was doing, but I knew if I just let go of the controls the aircraft would find her own level. I looked down. Yes, I'd hit the aiming point. And I could order the attack in. You see, by that time, I'd become so familiar with the whole technique that I could assess the position quickly, weigh one form of approach against another and act quickly but only because that had been my full-time job over a number of years. It still has a lesson for today, because if you want to be on top of what you're doing, live your job.

War taught me about interdependence. I mean I

was a pilot and I may have got the honours, but I knew the extent to which I depended on everybody down the chain of command. I was the CO,* and in that sense a slightly distant figure. But I was quite happy to have a drink with an airman, because I think that those under your command must respect you as a person. I don't think you break respect by meeting people on equal terms unless you're not up to it; if respect for you is based purely on the fact that you are the CO and a very good flyer and administrator, well a lot's missing.

The night in 1941 after my brother had been shot down I nearly made a fatal error. The Station Commander, Charlie Whitworth, my tutor at the Air Squadron, knew I always wanted to fly low level if I could and he said, 'Leonard, I've just thought of something. If you get over the target and shut your four engines down, you'll be able to come down low-level and nobody will know you're there.' (What we didn't know was that they already had radar, not just sound detectors.) I said that was a good idea. So we got over the target, Brunswick, and I shut my four engines down and got down lower and lower. Then I said to my engineer, 'We'd better do a check just to make certain,' because it was quite cold; 'let's just check if we can start one.' So we tried to start one and couldn't. I hadn't lost my head, I was quite calm, but we were getting lower and when we got to four thousand feet with no engines I said to my crew, 'I'm sorry, but you'll have to stand by to bale out.' I had a duty to them to give them a chance. And then suddenly the engineer realised I'd got my procedure wrong. I suppose my mind wasn't totally with it and I'd taken step two in front of step

* Commanding Officer

one. So he corrected me and suddenly both engines started on one side. Now the effect of that is to throw you into a violent spin. So I had a real struggle till we could get the other engines started, keeping her under control. Just before they started, when I'd said, 'Stand by to bale out!' my wireless op, Jock Hill, shouted out, 'Come on Sir, you can do better than that!' That remark's always stuck in my head. He said it nicely but firmly. And I think that shows something of the relationship in a crew. I was the boss; he was the sergeant, but you had the sort of relationship where a junior could pull you up if you needed a mental jerk.

I had to form my crew into a team, I had to make them know I cared for them, I had to look for what was good in them, for what was weak in them and to try and strengthen the weak and develop the good. You couldn't just sit there as pilot, you had to think of the rear gunner who was on his own, calling out now and then to make him realise you were thinking of him. You had to think about your ground crew and make them feel they were important to you and you would stand by them if they were in trouble. You had to see them as human beings, not just as a ground crew, because the way they serviced your aircraft was life and death to you. You went off and did your trip while they sat all night in a cold dispersal hut on the other side of the aerodrome. And when you landed six or seven hours later, you were debriefed, had your bacon and eggs and went back to bed, while they took the cowlings off and started working on the aircraft. So if you just said, 'Thanks very much,' and went off, you wouldn't have much of a relationship with them. And it was the same all the way through the station. There would be somebody who just swept the floor in the hangar, but it was crucial to you because it was keeping the dust off the aircraft. If you don't make people feel they are useful, you won't have such an effective unit.

And war gave me an insight into what men and women can achieve if they have a common goal, particularly if they understand the overriding importance of that goal. It taught me that money and personal satisfaction were not the ultimate thing, which is what I probably thought previously. I had the benefit of living and working with people who were setting me an extraordinary example. If you get credit for what you do, it's easy in a way but there are so many people who get none – and that's not only true in war. Particularly the 'little man' who is never seen, the unsung contributor. There were so many of them. I think of the scene before a bombing raid – an 'op' as we called it. There was a briefing session and as the CO, I would stand up on a little stage and detail the target for tonight – Berlin for example, and then the Intelligence Officer, the Met man* and others would give us information about the target and why it was important, the defences, the route, the estimated weather, the plan of action, how high we were going to fly, any special comments – and a few words of encouragement. I stood there and I looked at these seventy or eighty people all dressed more or less the same in battledress, and I thought that this was just one little unit amongst hundreds up and down Bomber Command, doing exactly the same thing at the same time. I could see clearly that a lot of them were worrying about the defences, while others were just thinking, 'Here's a target to attack and I'm going to get there and do it.' The latter were probably going to do a more

* Meteorological expert

spectacular job, but I think the former had the more difficult task and were braver. People talk about courage in war but courage can only exist if fear is there first; also, courage is a very subjective thing, we think of one man as brave and another as not, but we are judging from the outside.

The other thing is that courage depends on what's at stake. If somebody very precious to you is at risk, you will go through danger to help them, but the danger won't mean so much. But if it's something much less important to you, you won't have that concentration of mind and heart so you are much more likely to start thinking about the risks. If the objective you're going for isn't worthwhile at all, then the risk you are going through would be stupid and irresponsible, because the risk you take should be proportionate to the end you're seeking. Our Lord said, 'Where your treasure is, there will your heart be also' (Matthew 6:21). And that's true in every level of life.

The war taught me that there are times when you have to subordinate your own interests to the common good. And you realise that you are not doing it only for the common good but that your own good is bound up with it as well. In peacetime we don't quite see that to the same extent. If we recognised poverty and injustice in the world as an enemy in a similar way we saw the Nazis, we'd react very differently. And I think that is one of the sadnesses of life, that in war people go to such lengths to serve what they see as a common good. But when it comes to peacetime, we are all back following our own little goals.

All this sounds very positive, but in fact if you look objectively at what you were doing, you were conduct-

ing a form of warfare which, especially in retrospect, has become very controversial. The bombing obviously involved the deaths of thousands of innocent civilians. What about that side of it?

Let me start by putting it in its context. You see, if you take an isolated action, the bombing of a city, and say, 'How could you bomb innocent women and children?' you can't quite answer it. But what you've got to do is to put the bombing of that city in the whole historical context of the war. In 1940 the British Army was defeated, Europe was occupied and being rapidly turned into a virtually impregnable fortress. The Navy was fully stretched in keeping the vital Atlantic lifeline open, and only just by the skin of its teeth managed it. Had that been cut, we would have been finished. In any case, good military strategy demands that you counter-attack. Hitler had access to all the natural resources he wanted. So he was now rapidly building up an almost unbelievably powerful defensive and offensive force and it was absolutely crucial to take the war to him. And the only way that could be done, given we now had fortress Europe and no hope at all of penetrating that fortress, was over the top by air. The first intention was only to hit factories, but although I can testify to how hard we tried, it was impossible. You could not, at night in the European weather, with the navigation equipment we had, carry out that kind of precision attack. So it gradually became an area attack, in other words we bombed cities.

Once you come to modern war in built up areas like Europe, you can only conduct it at the price of enormous numbers of civilian casualties. Now you asked me how I can justify that. Well, I think the way I justify

it is this: if you take the bomber offensive as a whole
from 1940 to June 1944, it acted as the equivalent of a
second front, because of the huge resources in equipment and manpower Hitler had to divert from the bat-
tlefields to the defence of Germany. Furthermore, although the bomber offensive could not prevent German
war production rising, it could only rise at an enormous
cost to itself. Bomber Command destroyed more sub-
marines in the factories and on the way to the ports than
the Navy did in the whole Battle of the Atlantic, but,
most crucially of all, it won the air battle because it
forced the Luftwaffe to come up and fight and defeated
it. So when it came to D-Day, 6 June 1944, there wasn't
a single German aircraft over the beaches. Now, had
they been there the way they were at the Battle of
Britain, the landing wouldn't have succeeded. But for
the bomber offensive, there would have been no re-
entry into Europe in 1944 and I would defend that
against anybody.

Now then, you've got to look at what was happening in Europe. Apart from the fact that Hitler was
building up his massive striking force, he was setting
about the extermination of whole sections of the population: Jews, Gypsies, people he didn't like politically,
the handicapped. The elimination of the entire Polish
nation was also his goal. By the end of the war, he had
liquidated about twenty million people. That means
that every single day of the war, if you average it out,
approximately ten thousand men, women and children
were being put to death. So, if you are faced with that
happening, what is your duty? In my view, your duty is
clearly to end the war in the quickest possible time with
the minimum casualties. Now the bomber offensive
killed 500,000 civilians, but the totality of the war in

Europe killed 35 million civilians, 20 million in concentration camps and 15 million just in the land fighting. So against that background, I don't see what alternative there was to the bomber offensive.

If you'd let Germany go on unimpeded, she'd
have built up such military strength that she'd have
easily conquered the Russians and we could never have
touched her. She would have been free to do whatever
she wanted in Europe. We might have prevented her
invading North Africa, we might have prevented her
extending her borders, but we could never have done a
thing to help anybody inside Europe.

Now I'm not saying that we didn't make mistakes
– we did. One crucial mistake, but that was a mistake of
the High Command, was that, from the winter of 1944,
there was no adequate reason to go on bombing cities.
But the trouble is that in war, strategies and tactics that
have been successful over a period of years, have their
own inbuilt momentum. It takes a very flexible and
open mind to detect a change in the overall scene that
calls for a change in strategy. You launch this huge
monster which has got you out of trouble and then you
can't stop it.

*People often believe that you did a complete about-turn
after the war, that you felt the whole bomber offensive
had been the wrong policy and that guilt about your
role in the war was to affect what you did with the rest
of your life. From what you're saying, that doesn't seem
to be true. Though obviously you must have regretted it.*

I know they do. But I have to say that I don't have
a sense of guilt. You only feel guilty if you do something you know to be wrong. Of course I regret it

deeply, because who wants to be killing civilians? But I must repeat, there was no alternative. I did have a belief we could have bombed more accurately – on clear nights, not on cloudy nights – by a different form of marking. When I was posted to 617 Squadron, the Dambusters, we proved that with a specialised marking force, using a dive technique rather than a straight and level run-in one. Given clear weather, you could mark a target so accurately that your bombing could pretty well be confined to the target area. So I'm not convinced that we did it in the best way, but I am convinced it was the best way that Bomber Command as a whole could see. You are quite right, I regret it, but not in the sense that I wouldn't do it again were I back in the same situation. That anyone should seriously argue that we oughtn't to have fought Hitler is to me incomprehensible.

It's the paradox of war that the man in front of me is the enemy who is threatening the security and freedom, if not the existence, of the country he is attacking, but he is also a human being. In the First World War it happened that the enemy did something very human like dropping his trousers and relieving himself and the British side couldn't pull their triggers because they saw another human being doing an ordinary human act. But if they'd seen the enemy with a rifle in his hand, they'd have had no hesitation at all. In my case you could say, 'How could you drop bombs on civilians?' But I was thinking about the 10,000 a day dying in concentration camps. No, we didn't know the numbers but we knew about the gas chambers; we knew enough to know we were fighting an enemy who was evil through and through. Even if individuals didn't know, somebody knew.

But then you couldn't afford to think too much about civilians. You either had to do it or not do it. You couldn't afford to start hesitating, or you'd probably cause even more harm. And remember, when you're bombing and in the middle of very heavy flak, you don't see any human beings. You know perfectly well that you've got to focus your whole mind on getting through that opposition and dropping your bombs accurately and there isn't very much time to think about anything at all other than that. And you can't afford to let your mind dwell on casualties in war, whether they are the enemy's or those of your own unit. Doubt, as well as fear, is something you have to hold at bay.

There is one particular attack, the bombing of Dresden, undefended and full of civilian refugees, in February 1945, which is singled out nowadays as perhaps the hardest of all the Allied raids to justify. I know you weren't personally involved, but can you really say that this attack, too, was morally acceptable?

I think most historians would agree that the bombing of Dresden was a mistake, but it was a mistake made in good faith. There were a number of factors that led to the decision. One was that Dresden lay fifty or sixty miles directly ahead of the Russian advance and the Russians had asked for maximum bombing of all enemy strongholds on their path. Number two, there was an unconfirmed report that there was an armoured division reforming in Dresden. Number three, I don't believe that Bomber Command was aware of the number of refugees that were there or that all ack-ack had been removed from the city so there were no defences. More fundamentally still, the ME 262, the first jet fighter in the world, had appeared on the scene. There was talk of a revolutionary new midget submarine. If production of either of these was to increase dramatically, the course of the war might be changed. This too coloured the High Command's thinking. Now whereas in a normal attack over a heavily defended city, probably only forty per cent of the bombs would land in the city, a hundred per cent of the bombs landed on Dresden, so there was far more damage than would normally have been done. So all those factors contributed towards a decision made in good faith but a bad one. So I fully agree that the bombing of Dresden was a mistake, but I cannot agree with the assertion that it was a malicious act. If there's a finger to point it should be at the politicians who had it in their power to stop Hitler ever breaking out of Germany at all. However it's one thing to uphold the necessity of the offensive; it's another to claim that everything we did in it was right. You couldn't fight such a desperate war and not make mistakes and very bad mistakes. Soldiers make mistakes today just in a small encounter; they get enraged by something that's happened. If you see your son brutally killed in front of you, you're a very controlled human being if you don't feel a sense of anger against the attacker and want to go for him, and in a bigger scale that happens in war.

The war was a short period in your life, yet it obviously – and understandably – had an enormous effect on you; you often allude to it, even when you talk about your spiritual life. But some people might say you refer to it too much. Especially since, though you stress the positive effect it had on you, it can also bring out the worst in human values. So, what do you feel is the analogy between war and spirituality?

I'm wondering whether I've slightly – I don't mean overdone it, but failed to balance it by the other side, the human side. I can't leave this painful subject without acknowledging that I am stating the case as I see it from my limited perspective; only when the last judgement comes will we learn for certain the real right and the real wrong. Everything I've said is qualified by that realisation. But to come to your point about the analogy between war and spirituality. The problem whenever you're talking about the faith is that it's multifaceted and paradoxical – like Christians who just talk about the meek and mild Jesus – that's perfectly true, but there is a different side to him. If you make a statement about God and to a lesser degree about the spiritual life in the sense of his relationship with us, you immediately have to contradict it. You have to say that it is completely different from the way we understand it and I suspect that the difference is greater than the likeness. No matter what analogy you use and what truth it will contain, there's a whole area in which it is untrue. I have to point this out or people might get the wrong impression.

War is a theme running through Scripture and people liken it to a human war between armies, but it's self-evident that it isn't that type of war at all. There are similarities but there are dissimilarities. The war we're engaged in, the struggle to live the life that God wants for us and to live in total harmony with his wishes for us, is completely different from taking up arms and killing people, but it is nonetheless a struggle. I read about the drug barons in Colombia and I think what courage the judges and the police and the politicians who oppose them have, because they know the more they engage the drug barons, the more their safety as

well as the safety of their families is at stake. That drug
war is certainly interesting to Satan and his bad angels;
he must be very keen on seeing that the supply of drugs
is kept up and that as many people as possible are
brought into it and perverted, whereas a man who is
leading quite a good life and building up a good and
successful business or whatever, can't be of as much
concern to Satan. But first we must look to ourselves. If
I want to work for peace, my first job is to make certain
that the war in my own being is won, or at least that I
am doing as much as I can to win it.

*Isn't it a difficult thing to project though, this war
analogy? Especially in our western society when it no
longer seems exciting and dangerous to be a Christian?*

I think that, if we were really living, totally living,
our lives as Christians we would find that we were in
fact at war, but an unseen, mostly spiritual war. The
more deeply you lead a Christian life, the more in fact
you find yourself engaged in the struggle, the more you
become aware of the ultimate realities of life: the superficial realities, the physical realities of daily life,
start to disappear and you see that behind them are the
spiritual realities. You begin to see much more clearly
how sinful you are and how infinitely good God is, so
that immediately puts you into a state of tension. In
addition to that, you begin to discover the forces of evil
that are at work. The moment you start to pray, you
have to be prepared to conform your life to the differing
perception you receive on how to lead your life. You
begin to see that little things do count and the struggle
to improve yourself has in fact improved the whole of

humanity in a tiny way. It means that nothing you ever do is useless.

Your new project, the Memorial Fund is obviously very close to your heart. Again, though, isn't the Memorial Fund harking back to something that's past and gone? Especially as the enemy is now the friend, so to speak?

Yes, but I'm not remembering the war, I'm remembering those who died. My theme is 'Remember a life to save a life,' and I am convinced that it is that basic concept that makes it run. Forget the rights and wrongs of war; whichever side you were on, there would have been a family member or friend who died, and for the most part it was a young life lost. Some of the letters I've had from young and old have been incredibly moving. They speak of a personal loss: 'My beloved Jack.' Or it can strike a different chord. One girl of 25 wrote in and said, 'I know nothing about the war but somebody very close to me committed suicide because he was unemployed and felt he was useless, and I've agonised over this. Now suddenly you've given me a way of escaping from it, and I hope and pray that doing this will put his troubled spirit at rest.' Some people send money in thanksgiving that none of their family were killed. Somebody sent £76 'for the 76 years I've lived in Britain which has never been invaded'. The Fund is unusual, it's big, it's global, but it's also simple and eminently practical because the five pounds that the old lady or the young person gives is never lost. And I really think it corresponds to a genuine need in people's hearts.

I think one has to hold that our past is important. Forgetting whether it's war or peace, what we are today is because of what people were and did in the past, and likewise we contribute to the future. Now, fifty years on, we remember the spirit that drove those young men to leave their homes to fight and do what they perceived to be their duty. And the more we think about that, the more we must think about the need to mobilise ourselves in a similar kind of way but in the different circumstances of peace, to work against injustice. We look back in order to determine how we can do better for the future. We chose the whistle as our logo, because whistles were once used to send men into battle and we are now blowing them to call for help. That led to the idea of the 'Whistle Walk' in memory of the Battle of the Somme. School children walked sixteen-miles accompanied by a serving officer in full battledress. Sixteen miles was the length of the battle front for every yard of which, on the first day of the battle, one man was killed or maimed for life on the British side alone. It has proved not only popular and successful, but a kind of learning experience of the realities of World War One.

3
And peace

On 9 August 1945 an atomic bomb destroyed the port city of Nagasaki on Kyushu Island, southern Japan. It followed three days after a similar attack on Hiroshima. Casualty figures from the two attacks are uncertain but it has been estimated that well over 250,000 people died instantaneously and many more later.

Obviously your experience at Nagasaki was a major event in your life. To start with, did you and do you now feel such drastic action as the dropping of the atomic bombs on Japan was necessary or justified?

As a small part of the planning team for the invasion of Japan, I know there was no possibility of ending the war other than by invasion and total defeat of the home army. The Japanese at that time were under the control of a fanatical, military clique who were hell-bent on the total conquest of South East Asia, who looked upon civilians as second class citizens, and to whom surrender was the ultimate disgrace. The word did not even appear in the military code; you either died fighting or you committed hara-kiri.* The mistake that some people make when they're passing judgements on the atomic bomb is of applying western standards of thought to a regime that had a completely different way of thinking. That they faced inevitable defeat is perfectly true, but this didn't alter one iota their determination to fight it out to the last inch of soil and the last life. Now you know that the Japanese were occupying Burma, Malaysia, and the whole of Indochina. They'd built eight miles of underground tunnels for the defence of Singapore. Our planning team thought the war was going to last another eighteen months. And how many millions were going to die before they were defeated, no-one could possibly guess. The atomic bomb was the one hope of averting this catastrophe. CND** used to try and knock me down on this point, saying that it's not necessarily true that the Japanese would

* Ritual suicide by disembowelment
** Campaign for Nuclear Disarmament

have resisted invasion. But in war you can only act on the reality as in honesty you judge it to be; if an enemy picks up a gun and aims it at me, I've got to presume he proposes to fire.

Recently in Japan, I had dinner with a member of the Royal Family, who knew the principal personalities involved in the surrender decision. He was very western-orientated and very much against the military. I'd been longing to find someone who knew them, especially the Lord Keeper of the Privy Seal, the crucial negotiator between the Emperor and the military, and I asked whether it was true that one of the Inner Cabinet, the 'Big Six', who governed the country, had committed hara-kiri after the surrender declaration. 'Yes', he said, 'It was General Anami.'

'Did he commit ceremonial hara-kiri or just hara-kiri?'

A subtle change came over him and he said, 'Ceremonial hara-kiri... he did it beautifully.' Then, with his hands, he sketched out the action. There was no mistaking his respect for the act itself. It revealed in a way I had never before imagined how deep in their thinking it was that, rather than surrender, you committed hara-kiri, the dignified way in which you expunged the indignity of defeat. So the Americans were quite right; they had to demand unconditional surrender. They could allow the Emperor to remain, but they couldn't allow the imperial system because it was this system that gave the military their power. The military claimed that the Emperor was a god and that everything that they did in his name was therefore right, but he was never allowed to express an opinion contrary to theirs. That was where the terrible nature of that system lay. When, in June 1945, he convened an Imperial Conference and

said, 'I would like peace – not an order, just a wish,'
they were completely shattered. In his presence they
prostrated themselves. But when they got out of the
imperial chamber, they gave the order to fight on.

*You've already talked about it in the context of your
spiritual development but what were the feelings that
went on inside you during the actual mission?*

One thing I've never forgotten. Field Marshal
Maitland Wilson – called 'Jumbo' because he was a
very big man – said to me, 'Do you know what the
Atom Bomb is?' and I said: 'No Sir, I don't.' I could
see a look of relief on his face. Then he continued, 'In
order to minimise radiation' – that didn't mean anything to me – 'the bomb is set to explode two thousand
feet above ground', and he put his hands up and slammed
them down on the desk. Everything shook.

I walked back to my room, where the two other
officers dropped what they were doing and waited for
me to say something. They knew that nobody of my
rank was called directly by the Chief, so it had to mean
trouble or something dramatic. I gave them a nod,
collected my things, closed my desk and walked out. I
never went back to that office.

In San Francisco, I discovered a new side, perhaps
an efficient side, of the American way of doing things,
but not one that I liked. I was practically a number. I
was locked up in the base, not allowed off it and given
no indication of when I was going to be sent on, except
that I was handed a card with information punched into
it and told that, when the card fitted the machine, I
would be called.

We had something like a two-and-a-half day flight

with various stops to get to the island of Tinian in the Marianas and it was on that journey that I began to think that it was a turning-point in history, the possibility of a sudden end to World War Two. The day itself was full of problems and tension. Curtis Le May, the Strategic Air Commander, the big boss, had been determined that neither Bill Penney nor I should be on any atomic mission and had stopped us at the last moment from joining the Hiroshima flight. This time, we were pretty certain that we had outmanoeuvred him but, until an hour before the briefing, we still hadn't received official confirmation that we were on. The briefing itself was a fairly solemn business. This was the last bomb the Americans had – anyway for six weeks or so – and if it didn't succeed in making the Japanese surrender, the massive campaign to reconquer South-East Asia would have to go ahead. Then the height we were flying at, thirty thousand feet, worried me. I know it doesn't sound logical, but, over Germany, the odds were against us: out of every twenty aircraft, one was lost, on average, in every raid. Somehow this made me feel it was a fair fight. But here we were above flak and out of reach of fighters. I can't explain it, but it felt not quite right. I was decidedly uncomfortable.

After about six hours of flight, we hit the Japanese coast and began to fly parallel with it. I was struck by how beautiful it looked in the early morning sunshine. It suddenly reminded me of Cornwall, in particular of a night when we had attacked Brest and had a very rough time. We came back and hit the lovely Cornish coast and I can still remember that lovely feeling – Britain! We're home! Looking down at Japan, that memory came back to me and I thought, 'What am I doing? As a boy I said I never wanted to go to war, I couldn't see the

sense of war. And here I am part of a mission that's
going to kill I don't know how many tens of thousands
of people. I must have gone mad.' Then of course the
other side came into play, 'Yes, but we're at war, I
know what's at stake and this is the last bomb we've
got.'

I was in plane number three and my pilot diso-
beyed orders by flying 9000 feet higher than he should
have done because he thought it was safer. And instead
of doing a circle around Yakushima, the little island
that we were to rendezvous over, he was doing forty
mile dog-legs, so we didn't meet up with the other
aircraft. This put the unfortunate Charles Sweeney, the
lead pilot, at great risk because he had to wait for us and
was short of fuel. So things were going wrong with the
attack all the way along. The primary target, Kokura,
was obscured and had to be abandoned because the
orders were to drop on a visual or not at all. Sweeney
then turned to Nagasaki, the secondary target, but there
was radio silence so we couldn't be sure of this and my
pilot was wondering what to do. I was indignant that he
was flying too high, for I'd never known a pilot not fly
the height he was ordered to, especially on this sort of
attack. But there was nothing I could do to persuade
him to come down. Then he suddenly announced that
he was going to abandon the attack, saying, 'Look, we
don't know where they are, let's go back.' I half ex-
ploded, 'We've come all this way, right across the
Pacific, years building the bomb, months of training,
and now, at the very last minute, you're going to give it
up!' and he said, 'OK we'll go on for a bit.' But, left to
himself, he would have gone back!

So when it went off we weren't where we should
have been, which was right on the pilot's tail; we were

about forty miles away and were caught by surprise. We had dark glasses to look at the flash, but of course they weren't on. In the bright sunlight of nine o'clock in the morning, there was a flash in the cockpit and we instantly knew that that was the bomb. We turned round towards it and there was this incredible sight in the sky. It was a black cloud, no, not black, probably grey. It was, I estimated, about half a mile in diameter but what was extraordinary about it was that it was bubbling, like a cauldron. First there had been a flash which we only saw out of the corner of our eyes, then there was a fire, a red hot fire, which then cooled down into this cloud, I can only describe it as a cloud, but the heat in it must have been I don't know what. I know that, at the moment of detonation, it was approaching the heat of the sun. We'd been well-briefed what to expect, but seeing it was a different experience altogether. The cloud was rocketing upwards with enormous speed and getting bigger as it did so, but underneath it, as if linking it to Nagasaki, was a column of cloud gently spiralling; it was whiter than the huge sphere balanced on top. What struck me most was that the whole thing was so symmetrical. You see, I was used to high explosives going off and they've got no shape; they're frightening, but they're ragged. This had a shape almost as if sculpted and that gave me a much greater feeling of power. Like the difference between an angry man out of control whom you can probably cope with and the angry strong man who is completely under control. But then other emotions began to take over. I think my first conscious thought was, 'It's the end of the war;' the longer I looked at that thing, the more I thought, 'That's a weapon you cannot fight.' This led to a feeling of intense relief; all the tension of the war suddenly seemed to be released. Then again I said, 'Come on, you've got a job to do, think, what about the points you've got to write down.' So I struggled to apply my mind to that.

Now the next thing that caught my attention was at the base of that column, where it fanned out into a pyramid which must have been two miles across at the bottom. The intense heat had set fire to houses and anything else combustible and the ashes and dust were being sucked up into the air and that pyramid was completely black. And I thought, 'Inside that cloud are people!' I've talked about it before, this paradox of war. When you're young, you want to live, you want others to live, but the enemy has got to be defeated, so you have this horrible swinging backwards and forwards.

Another thought was that this was only the beginning of a whole new age. If that was the first bomb, what was the atom bomb of fifty years' time going to be like? In fact on the way back, when it was all over and we were sitting quietly and sort of ruminating, Bill Penney said, 'That's only the detonator for the real bomb that we're only beginning to work on'. He meant the hydrogen bomb. Those can't have been his exact words, but that's what stuck in my mind. That bomb symbolised the whole horror of World War Two, and at the same time gave me a fleeting, hazy vision of what a future war would be if it were ever fought.

Nagasaki is frequently portrayed as a turning-point in your life. But what sort of a turning point was it?

For me, it was the end of world war. Having seen the atomic bomb, I could not believe that nations that held the bomb could ever fight each other. I looked at

that dreadful sight over Nagasaki and I said, 'If the
enemy's got that bomb, you just can't fight him. He
puts that down on your cities and then what?' I was
totally convinced that, so long as each side kept an
effective deterrent, there would be no war.

As I continued to ponder it over the years, I became totally convinced that this is true: war between
nuclear powers is not a rational option of state policy.
And when the peace movements argue, 'But governments aren't rational, look at the way wars got started
in the past,' I say, 'Yes, I quite agree, but the one area in
which they are rational is that they want to stay in
power. So for them to take a step that's going to destroy
them, is not conceivable. They can only do that on a
judgement that the other side would never respond, so
as long as each side keeps a credible deterrent, then in
my view there is never any possibility of war.'

Add to that the complete volte-face in public attitudes to major war. Throughout recorded history, war
was the accepted way of solving your differences or
achieving your national objectives. Battle was a glorious thing. Governments knew the people were behind
them. And for the most part, governments sent their
armies out to fight while they stayed at home. When it
came to 1914, the same view prevailed, and so they
didn't hesitate to take that first, crucial step that set in
motion the events which led to the First World War.
But weapons had become so powerful that there was no
longer any mobile fighting; armies were tied down in
trenches and as that war progressed, attitudes began to
change. It had started with euphoria – the vast, cheering
crowds in front of Buckingham Palace. My father had
been rushing to try and stop mother catching a train to
go to France – they were engaged then – and got caught

up in a crowd, all shouting, laughing and waving. There
was an old woman there, wringing her hands and saying, 'They don't know what they are doing.' By 1916
with the Somme, there was a completely different attitude and by the end of the war, disillusionment, anger,
resentment had set in so that, instead of a victory parade on Armistice Day in 1919, which had always been
the case in the past, there was a peace parade. People
were shocked by the inhuman aspect of that war. Well,
that had an unfortunate consequence, because, when it
came to Hitler in 1938, the public attitude and in particular the government attitude was, 'Anything other
than war – let's give into him, he can't really be as bad
as he looks.' But that was exactly what Hitler wanted;
so that excessive fear of war brought about the very
catastrophe we had sought to avert. I don't know what
would have happened if we'd stood firm in 1938, but I
know there wouldn't have been a world war.

Every generation wants peace. People probably
want peace in the sense of freedom to pursue their own
lives; it's not a totally selfless peace. But the historical
and social circumstances of each generation differ. My
generation had a war. I was brought up in the aftermath
of World War One and I could never understand how
men could go through all that and still keep going.
Compared with life in the trenches, my war was nothing, I've no illusions about that. In the early 1930s,
though I was a member of the Cadet Corps, the effect
of the First World War was to make me say, 'I reject
war.' But then, once Hitler came, especially after Munich, we realised that there couldn't be peace in Europe
until he was stopped. So we were working for peace
within the historical framework that we were set, and
the only way we could work for peace was to win, but

not just to win, to win in such a way that we ended up
with a better peace, or at least the circumstances under
which a better peace could be built. At the end of
World War One, the politicians had done the reverse.
They had created a peace treaty which, in some of its
elements, was manifestly unjust to the Germans, so
when Hitler came to power, he was able to feed on that
grievance and it gave him a power base.

At the end of World War Two then, the combina-
tion of the sheer, devastating power of the weapon and
the realisation that appeasement didn't work, put us
into a completely new age of history, in which war
between major nations is now an impossible option. Of
course you can't say it's physically impossible, but I
would say that it's in fact impossible, and I would
argue that the Superpowers know it and they are clearly
moving away from that position. They've acknowl-
edged to each other that they can't afford to fight each
other.

*But the anti-nuclear movements argue that the present
climate in Eastern Europe – and the reduction of weapons – is largely a victory for them.*

Yes, I know they do. But I think it's a victory for
reality, for the fact that we didn't drop our guard. Had
we given everything away, the Soviets would have
been in such a strong position that they might conceiv-
ably have called any tune they wanted. I was always
concerned about peace building , but I saw a very great
threat to peace in the peace movement and therefore I
felt that, as I had been involved in the atomic bomb,
that was something I had to take up. Because if they
won that argument, things might have turned out very

differently indeed. I won't say that they would have done, but they might have done. But in a sense, the peace movement did serve a purpose in emphasising the need to work for peace.

Is the deterrent theory something about which you've altered your thinking at all – especially in view of the disarmament process and the apparently reduced threat from the Soviet Union? Or are you worried by the fact the West may be lulled into a, possibly false, sense of security?

Justifying the nuclear deterrent isn't such an issue to me now as it's become clear how it's serving its purpose between the Superpowers. But that doesn't mean the end of war. Other Hitlers will appear and hold the world to ransom. When the Gulf Crisis broke out, I felt we had learned a lesson from the past: hold together and don't at any price appease. Though one major criticism was that our intelligence wasn't good enough; we should have been better prepared.

I still think it's necessary to have a deterrent always and at every level. The police force is a deterrent, and I've never heard anybody say, 'Things have changed, let's do away with the police force.' It wouldn't get public support because people see muggers on the streets. You've now got the situation where a small country can hold a superpower at ransom, by terrorist attacks against any of its installations, even its ordinary citizens. People talk about total disarmament, but what do they actually mean? Are they going to allow shotguns? Are they going to allow knives? Since the beginning of the human story, millions and millions have been killed, still are, with knives, batons, rifles and so

on. A weapon is not immoral in itself, it's the use to
which it's put. I'm inclined to think that, the less powerful the weapon, the easier it is for people to assume
they can get away with violence. I don't believe that
human nature has changed, not to the extent that there
will never be men of violence. That's hardly conceivable. So the nature of the deterrent will change according to the weapons. To us, the nuclear bomb is the most
powerful thing the world has ever known, but we don't
know what's coming tomorrow.

We tend to think that all that technology has given
us is a vastly more destructive weaponry. But new
technology has also given the terrorist far more power
to strike his selected target by remote control. These
huge armaments are effective as between the two Superpowers; they can deter, or if necessary, defeat, a
smaller nation on the battlefield, but I don't see that
they can prevent terrorism, hijacking or kidnapping.
For that, we should change our military thinking and be
putting far more money and resources into rapid de-
ployment forces, counter-intelligence, counter-insur-
gency, under-cover operations, finding out in advance
what the other man is intending to do. I really fear we
are entering an era which will see a fundamental change
in the nature of armed conflict, a kind of return to the
nomadic technique. The nomad had no defence if attacked by a larger group, but said, 'If you kill me, my
family will kill ten of yours.' The Mosaic law, which
we judge harsh, reduced this to one for one – an eye for
an eye. So today, defeat on the battlefield may well be
avenged by continuing acts of terrorism against soft,
defenceless targets anywhere and everywhere. To coun-
ter this effectively, the world community will need to
close ranks; the separate terrorist groups are clearly

closing ranks themselves, willing to exchange expertise and weaponry and, I suspect, to act on each other's behalf. All the more reason to keep an appropriate deterrent, I mean appropriate to the circumstances and the military capability of the aggressor nation. It's not a harmful thing having a deterrent; look how it worked to the mutual advantage of the Superpowers.

But I wonder how you can reconcile your views on defence and your argument that the bombing campaign, which killed thousands of innocent people, was justified, with, say, your strong opposition to abortion. Some people might see something incongruous there. If you say killing may be done in a legal framework sanctioned by the state – well, abortion is legal, isn't it? How would you, personally, interpret the commandment, 'Thou Shalt not Kill'? And for that matter, Christ's exhortation to 'Turn the other cheek.'?

It's perfectly clear that you must not kill – and I know you could look upon me as a dubious man to say this in view of the amount of killing I've been involved in – but the commandment must surely be interpreted as meaning you must not kill without lawful reason. True, a person who kills her unborn child may be acting within the law, but I would say that killing becomes lawful, in the profound sense, not in the legalistic sense, only when its purpose is to stop somebody killing others.

If it's I myself who is being attacked, it may be a counsel of perfection that I turn the other cheek (cf Matthew 5:43-48) and allow myself to be killed but if the aggressor is killing someone else, or worse still, a whole group of others, then it cannot be a counsel of perfection for me to refrain from going to their defence. The peace movement says we have a duty to love our neighbour and therefore, even if someone has a gun, I may not shoot him. But if I'm faced by two groups of people, the one killing the other and the other innocent victims, my clear duty in charity is to defend the victims.

If you're a policeman on duty in a crowded airport lounge and a terrorist pulls out a submachine gun and is opening fire, you can't say that you would not be allowed to shoot that terrorist. You would have to hold that, under those conditions, it was your duty to shoot. If possible you should disable, rather than kill, but in the rough-and-tumble of that kind of situation, that's virtually impossible. Even suppose you couldn't be sure of not hitting civilians in the process, I still don't think you could hold your fire, because every second you did so, the more people would die. In my view it's lawful not only because the government's given you that instruction, but because its purpose is to stop killing.

It's very noticeable that if you put the gunman scenario before a pacifist, he is far less confident and says something like, 'I'd fling myself between him and those he is shooting,' which just means another corpse. Lord Soper,* a committed pacifist and most sincere Christian, answered me on television, 'I need to know a lot more about what his motives are, how he was brought up, what his relationship is to the people, to enable us to try and talk him round .' I said, 'It might be a bit late, Lord Soper.' The point is, if the pacifist says, 'You may not shoot', he loses his credibility because people clearly see you've got to do something. And if he says, 'Well,

* Former president of the Methodist Conference

in that particular instance, I'd shoot because it's only
two or three lives,' he's ceased being a total pacifist and
become a relative pacifist. When it's reduced to something that's very human and personal and close to you,
the issue is much clearer. The pacifist's strength comes
from the fact that he talks about world war and millions
of deaths, far removed and on such a vast scale that it's
harder to grasp.

*But you seem to have a rather pessimistic view of
human nature – hat in order to stop killing we have to
resort to killing... It seems a gloomy scenario for the
future of the world.*

In the past, war was so much a part of the international scene that people took it for granted and apart
from the Church's attempts at defining a 'just war',
didn't bother much about its morality. Now suddenly
that's changed in respect of the major nations, but they
still have their goals and ambitions, so they're going to
have to pursue those in different ways. That raises all
sorts of interesting questions. For instance, one of the
ways in which the Church allowed you to go to war was
to correct a gross injustice in another part of the world.
Nowadays, if one nation invades, occupies and op-
presses another nation in an area under the control of
another Superpower, as was the case in the Second
World War with Germany, you can no longer do that.
In a sense, injustice has become institutionalised in that
you can't now use armed force to correct it from the
outside. So I feel we're moving into a whole different
area of life that's going to pose new problems. I don't
know what those problems are, but I can see that the
struggle is still going to be as fierce. If you're going to

struggle for justice, and the simple way of dealing with an oppressive regime, by overthrowing it by force, is now denied you – how are you going to do it? And selfishness, to a greater or lesser extent, is still going to dominate human actions. We're going to have different forms of violence: terrorism, subversion, threats, violent crime, football hooliganism, violence from little pressure groups who think they've got a cause or an injustice to put right, people who just think violence is clever. And fundamentalism in its more extreme forms unquestionably has the drive and commitment that could well unite the nation, or the members of a particular grouping behind a leader bent on aggression.

Now, a deterrent keeps war at bay, but simply keeping war at bay doesn't give you peace. Peace has to be built, patiently, but with a total commitment. We need not only to be prepared, we should see as the highest priority of all the eradication of injustice in all its forms. The real lesson of 1939-45 is that each of us should be working in whatever way we can to remove the root causes of war and that means working to establish, improve and safeguard human rights, working against repression – and making certain we don't look for too much for ourselves to somebody else's detriment, which is of course the most difficult thing to do of all!

I think Pope John Paul II put it most concisely when he said 'the primary cause of war is excessive self-interest'. You start off by wanting to better yourself and your family. That's good. But then you think you'll go a step further and gradually you find that, to keep going, you've got to outdo other people. You get competitive and advance your own interests with the result that others have got to drop back. Before long, you find that people are in your way and you have to push them out of your way because advancement has become an obsession. Then ultimately you end up by actually disliking the people that are poor, despising them because they haven't got money, taking it out on them because they're a reproach to you. It seems to me that, once you set your sights on money, power comes with it. The danger is that the love of money is linked to an inbuilt knowledge that we have been created to transcend ourselves, that we are something greater than what we actually are. It's true we are made to transcend ourselves, but by becoming sharers in God's life, not, by seeking self-aggrandisement, or getting all sorts of possessions which are an extension of ourselves. They may give you greater influence, greater power, but it's the wrong transcendence.

Even in the most austere man, there can be a point beyond which he's not prepared to give. And I'm looking at myself as well as other people; I have a nagging, persistent feeling that there is a vested interest lurking in me, an ego, the sum total of all the attachments I don't want to let go of, that demands its rights and wants recognition. I can't quite identify it, but I've got the feeling that, if it were attacked, I would react very angrily, strongly, perhaps even roughly. It comes back to me in dreams. I just feel that there's something inside me that's determined to protect my little castle.

Now, more often than not, people judge issues from a certain standpoint and this is particularly noticeable in abortion. Those in favour of abortion have got their eyes fixed on the mother and her needs and wishes. If having that child is going to spoil her life, then she should be free to decide that she's not going to have that child; that to them seems a perfectly good and just point of view. They're not doing it out of malice, they're doing it because they genuinely think that's correct. The other side are looking at the little unborn child and they are saying, 'This is a human life, which the mother, together obviously with somebody else, has brought into being and its life needs to be protected. To take its life for no adequate reason is unlawfully killing a helpless person.'

I've noticed how people can protest violently against other forms of killing and even against selling arms to Third World nations for non-aggressive purposes, their argument being the iniquity of taking innocent life. OK, arms sales are a complex issue, I'm not sure I know the answer, but when I say, 'What about killing the unborn child?' there's fury, 'How can you compare the two?' But who is more innocent or helpless than the unborn child? Their eyes are closed to that. They're not thinking about killing, just about the mother's right to determine what she wants. And if she's only thinking of her own convenience, that right is suspect because it's a selfish right, isn't it? If she's saying, 'I don't want that child to live because that poor child will be handicapped,' I agree that her case sounds much stronger. But my forty-two years amongst disabled people have shown me how much they have to give us. If a mother doesn't want a handicapped child, there are plenty of places that could be found for him. To destroy him is for me a terrible thing.

How easily the judgements of even good-intentioned people can be swayed was dramatically demonstrated in a recent House of Commons debate* about a case of accidental food poisoning that had

* The Food and Water Safety Act, 21 February 1989

caused the death of an unborn child. The Nine o'clock
BBC News reported that, 'Before a shocked and silent
House,' a leading front-bench read out a letter from the
mother, in which she said she felt both guilty and a
victim – because she had caused her child's death by
eating the food, but hadn't had the necessary information to safeguard it. If they are so shocked by an accidental killing, how is it that they are not even more
shocked at the intentional killing of the unborn child?
How is it that the pro-abortionist, who defends so vehe-
mently the mother's right to kill if she so wishes, now
suddenly takes the opposite view? Only because he was
not fighting his corner, his guard was down and so he
was judging more objectively.

Incidentally, you remember that I talked about
Catholics being a disappointment – and I find it a bit
disappointing to see, when it comes to the abortion and
embryo experimentation debates in the House of Lords,
which go to the very heart of our Catholic faith, how
few Catholic peers and peeresses take part. I really
think that Catholic peers ought to take it more seriously. If you accept the honour of a peerage, then I
think you've got to live your duties. The same goes for
the Anglican bishops, most of whom are conspicuously
absent.

It's true that the law permits abortion up to a
certain point. That makes it legal but it doesn't make it
moral. The state is not the determiner of morality. We
need to make that big distinction there and it's a dilemma that faces all states. If, therefore, a law is passed
that permits you to kill an unborn child, then those who
have no faith and sadly even some who have a faith,
will be convinced that they are operating lawfully and
need not worry. Well then it falls upon the members of

the Church to do all in their power to convince the lawmakers and the public as a whole that there's an error. We have to do it gently and with great understanding because most of those people are acting in good faith. It's often been said that one should distinguish between the individual who's trying to act for the best and the error or the sin.

The mentality that takes such a stand on, say, the arms issue, while feeling so differently about destroying the unborn child could be similar to the way people pontificate and pontificate about things on the other side of the ocean, but have a different view when it's something on their own doorstep. It's a complete contradiction, for example, to condemn the way the Americans put up trade barriers and the way the multinationals profiteer out of the countries they work in and then to say that trade barriers against Indian textiles are absolutely right and proper. The sad thing is that we don't see how self-interest rebounds against us because our own interest is bound up with the common good. An Indian Minister of Finance once said to me, 'You in the West will end up so wealthy that you have nowhere to sell any of your goods.'

We're all created to love and love is a great energy flowing outwards to its object. The question is, what do we love? Either we love God and our neighbour, or we turn that love back into ourselves so that energy is just going round and round and dragging everything into us like a black hole in space.

4

Lessons of
the disabled

'The history of the treatment of the sick and disabled is illuminated by the flashing humanity of a handful of reformers and innovators. Leonard Cheshire joins that select group for the world-wide network of Homes which he has managed to establish in the face of every kind of difficulty and discouragement. It is one of the greatest acts of humanity of our time.'

HRH the Duke of Edinburgh

*Arthur Dykes was to be the first of the disabled people
you looked after. But how did you come to take him in?
And how did you cope? After all you didn't have any
knowledge of nursing.*

I thought it couldn't be difficult to find somewhere for him. Arthur had been a nursing orderly in the
Air Force; in the post-war years everything was done
for ex-servicemen and we had a National Health Service. But the moment they heard he didn't need treatment, nobody would have him, except a private nursing
home, and that was ten pounds a week. Arthur had
twenty-seven shillings and sixpence a week* and I only
had my pension. So I said to him, 'Would you like to
come back to Le Court?' Well, I didn't honestly think
he would, because there was an empty house and only
me, but he somewhat startled me by saying, 'Yes, I'd
love to!' I rang the local District Nurse and said, 'What
am I going to do now?', so she came around on three
evenings and gave me what she called a concentrated
course on nursing, and I took Arthur in. We shared the
next three months together. It was a large twenty-five-
bedroom house with no electricity because the electric
plant we had had broken down. I only had three or four
oil lamps. It was cold but it was May, so it didn't
matter.

And soon there was another patient, who came to
me from the porter of a block of flats in which my aunt
lived. I used to go and visit my aunt who had quite a
habit of telling me what I ought or ought not to be
doing. She disapproved strongly of what I was up to
and didn't see the point of it – she thought I should

* £1.37½p

either stay in the Air Force or go into business. So I used to have a cup of tea with the porter downstairs before going up to her. And my aunt told him one day how awful it all was, how I was wasting my time and had thrown away a good career. Now I'm sure this porter totally agreed with what she was saying, but he also thought, 'There's the solution for my grandmother-in-law!' So he phoned me up and said, 'She's ninety-one, living in a fifth storey flat, her husband's died and nobody's looking after her. Will you take her?' Before I knew what I was doing, I said yes. So he said, 'What do I do? Fill out a form?' and I said, 'No, just send her!' And the London County Council ambulance brought her down to Le Court the next day. I can still see her, fully dressed and with a big pheasant's feather in her hat, as they carried her in on a stretcher. Wondering if they'd come to the right place, they got inside the huge building, which was completely empty – that morning I'd had to dash out to borrow sheets and blankets because I'd sold everything to pay the debts – and took her up and put her on the bed. I looked at Granny and said, 'This is not going to be quite as simple as Arthur...'

My mother used to send me things over. Of course she and my father would like to have seen me stop all this. And I kept thinking, 'Have I gone mad? I'm just an old, finished pilot – what am I doing?' I used to go through a real crisis of confidence. I used to look at the gardener and say, 'He knows what he's doing but I don't'.

How did you feel about Arthur in the initial days? Did you resent him perhaps?

No, I was very fond of him. It was a challenge, you see – though I might have felt a bit sore that the

state did nothing for him. I would read marvellous
statements by Cabinet Ministers: 'We do everything
for you for the rest of your life,' and here was a man in
clear need, and they wouldn't even touch him. No, he
was a man I liked and he was a human being. As far as
I was concerned, he and the others were people whom I
hadn't sought, but they were there and there was no
alternative I could find for them. I felt, 'Well, God has
put them in my way and so long as I don't choose
whom I'm taking, but take those who are in front of me,
whose need is self-evident and for whom there is literally nowhere else to go, then I can safely go ahead.' So
when the doctor came and told me I was being completely irresponsible: 'You've no idea what you're doing and you've no right to do it', I said, 'Well, doctor,
you suggest an alternative and if you can find an alternative I'll gladly send them away.' But that didn't
convince him – he just went on at me!

*It sounds almost unbelievably unselfish of you. Did you
see it as a bit of an adventure – or did you perhaps see
it as helping you?*

I didn't think that deeply. I just felt it was something that had to be done. Furthermore, like in the war, I
had no time to think. I had up to twelve people to look
after without any assistance. Some of them needed help
in the night, so I had to put my mattress outside their
doors and give them a handbell and if they rang, I'd get
up and do whatever they needed as best I could. There
was one who was slightly niggling – he used to wake
me up in the night and say, 'Will you put your hand on
my tummy and tell me if I ought to go to the loo!' But I
was young – thirty going on 31 – I had nothing else that

I wanted, and at first I just looked on it as a little interlude – once it was finished I'd go off and find my great career you see.

When I was in my somewhat over-pious period, it was external circumstances and people who brought me down to earth. For instance I had the lawn to keep cut. There were about two acres of it and I only had an Atco, which meant I couldn't let the grass grow too high or I'd never be able to cut it, so I used to have to dash out and spend a couple of hours at the mower keeping the lawn under control. I knew that, once I let it get ahead of me, I was sunk. There was a very big kitchen-garden – that and the flower gardens used to employ twenty-one gardeners before the war. I kept two of the gardeners on and paid their wages and sold the vegetables and flowers in Alton each week. That gave me the money to buy food. Arthur gave me his weekly National Assistance money, minus what he wanted for his cigarettes.

In the early days at Le Court I got the residents – I called them patients then – to help in the household chores. There were oil-lamps to be trimmed and so on. Granny got a bucket of potatoes and she was told to peel them, which she refused to do, so I cooked them in their jackets and she didn't like that so she soon obeyed! I had quite a tough time with her because she'd been a district nurse when she was young and was perpetually telling me that I was doing everything in the wrong way. She wouldn't let me take her stockings off so I could wash her feet. And she was stone deaf. When she didn't want to hear something, she didn't hear it, no matter how hard you shouted and when you said something that had nothing to do with her in a whisper, you could be sure she would pick it up. But we ended up with quite an affectionate relationship. One day she suddenly flung her arms round my neck, kissed me and said, 'I love a young man'. And I said, 'I love an old lady!'

Arthur was extremely independent-minded. When he arrived, he wouldn't even let me carry him up the stairs, so he sort of laboriously went up, with me with an arm round him pretending not to help him. In a way, it led to his death – he wouldn't have a bedpan so we went through the awful business of my leading him across the floor to the commode and it was while I was helping him back that he suddenly gave a groan and half collapsed. Instead of just relaxing with him, I picked him up and carried him to bed and it was in picking him up that he had a haemorrhage. It was a good lesson for me because it taught me very quickly that disabled people want their independence. You tend to think 'Well there he is, I must look after him, he's just lying there.' It's a commentary on life really, as Father Clarke used to say to me, 'You don't reach heaven on a feather bed.'

But do you think that, if Arthur had come your way before you started thinking about God, you would have had the same reaction?

I think that, without faith, I would still have responded. I know compassion is not usually associated with war, but I'd found great compassion in it. For one thing, you recognise how fragile you are. You may be as skilled, as tough, as fearless as anything, but it's not you who govern whether you come through or not. The sky is full of shells and you don't know where they're going to burst. Yes, you can cut down on some of the

errors that could finish you, you can minimally reduce
the likelihood of your being shot down and you have a
duty to acquire the skills, experience and mental outlook to bring you through if it's humanly possible, but
in the last resort, it's down to what the non-believer
would call luck and I would call Providence. You become very aware of that as you see so many of your
friends shot down and not coming back. People say
young men are just aggressive and like nothing more
than to have a gun in their hands and start shooting, but
I think that's absolute nonsense. They're not just shooting, they're being shot at and I'd like to know what
young man likes to be in the middle of gunfire and
bursting bombs. I think most writers will say they found
compassion in the war and you certainly learned to be
compassionate towards your own people. I don't see
how you can walk away from a man who's dying and
doesn't know what to do with his future. I don't think
you could go away and live with yourself very easily.

Except that some other people could easily do that...

Well, if they had a family to bring up...you see I
was on my own then. I'd had a wartime marriage that
had not survived my time in America and I had no
obligations, so I was a bit different. I knew I didn't
want to go into a moneymaking career; I knew I didn't
want to go into politics. I couldn't see the point of
staying in the Air Force as we'd had a war to end wars.
I just felt inwardly that there was something for me to
do and I think that everybody who's got an aim, whether
big or small, that's special to them, starts with that
inner feeling that somewhere there's something for them.
But they can't identify it, so they keep shouting, 'This
is it. No it isn't, it's that', and friends and family say,

'Can't you settle down and be sensible and take a steady job?' They don't see that there's something driving them inside until eventually a little door opens and they say, 'That's my door!' Well I didn't think Arthur was my door, but the time came when I realised he was.

How did you start turning your driving force into a structured organisation?

Le Court filled up and up and up. It got to the point where I could no longer run it, not in the sense that I couldn't put in the man hours, but I just didn't know how to organise it. And I felt – you've probably never felt it – absolute despair. I longed to see the place organised and with a structure but didn't know how to begin. I was compelled to do something and being an Englishman, I formed a committee. And one of the first things they said was, 'You've got to understand that money is the key to the problem; you just cannot run a nursing home without money. So now you've appointed us we will close the nursing home down and we will organise a good appeal and we'll get the money in the bank and set off on the right foot.' So that was agreed. Then somebody said, 'What do we do with the twenty-two patients?' And they couldn't sort that one out, so they said they would defer it to the next meeting – and so they kept deferring the problem of where to send twenty-two patients who wouldn't be there anyway if there was somewhere for them to go! And the day came when they said, 'It's a funny thing – we haven't got any money, but it still seems to be running!' I was really pleased at that. The other extraordinary thing concerned my £18,000 worth of debts. At the time when I took Arthur in, I didn't have much time to think about pay-

ing off the debts, I just continued selling everything I
had and from that moment on, the debts just disappeared.

But how on earth could that happen?

Well I mean, as a religious man, I'd say this was
what God wanted me to do and he would provide the
help I couldn't find myself. If I had decided to start a
nursing home of my own accord, then I couldn't expect
Providence to help me. That's been my built-in fundamental policy. I will never initiate anything of my own
will – although there have been times when I've been
persuaded to. I will only react to what's happening. It
doesn't mean we're not pro-active in a certain sense –
once you've determined a need you've got to organise
a strategy to meet it. But, as I told our Trustees at their
meeting last weekend, we should only have a strategy
for what we can see is a need that other people are not
meeting. Now what I call the theoreticians don't like
that, and they attack me for it. They say I should sit
down and plan, and I say, 'No, let's just react to need
and start small and grow and adapt ourselves as we go
because we can't tell what will happen. Draw up a great
plan and it may be wrong.'
At Predannack, I took one of the derelict buildings
on the aerodrome, the ex-station headquarters which
was in a terrible state. It had been unoccupied for five
years or more and it had the Cornish wind sweeping
over the Lizard peninsula. I wrote to the Air Ministry
and said I wanted the building for these disabled people
– I knew I wouldn't get an answer for seven months at
the very earliest and if I was well installed by then they
wouldn't be able to turf me out! So I put this fellow –

the epileptic boy – to trying to get it restored but he wasn't really much of a worker. Anyhow it meant that I got that old building, which not only didn't have any electricity, it didn't even have any drains. But I and a gradually growing band of helpers got round that problem. I got a huge old tank that was lying around, longer than this room and dug a great hole and sunk it in and connected it up to the drains and so started a second Home.

Many people find it very difficult to talk to the disabled. It's probably especially hard to know how to approach someone who's suddenly helpless after having been fit and healthy. How do you go about it?

I think you need to try and understand something of the inner rebellion that must take place in a formerly able-bodied person who becomes disabled, that says, 'Why me?' There are very few who don't experience it. And if you want to help, the worst thing you can do is to ignore that, pretend it doesn't exist, pretend there's no disability and say things like, 'What a lovely view you've got,' or 'What films do you like?' and so on.

I find disabled people all so different. With some, I feel I can instantly say, 'John, would you mind telling me what happened?' With others it takes longer. Though I think that nearly every disabled person likes it if you ask them how they got their disability, as long as they feel you're sincere. Because not many people do it. Princess Margaret is particularly good at saying, 'What happened to you?' and they feel quite honoured. Then I can go on to ask about their feelings and difficulties. Now there are other people who obviously haven't come to terms with their disability. With them, I've got to be quite different. I don't think I could say there's any standard way to approach them, except making myself available, finding some common ground, where they realise that I'm not being there just because I want to be compassionate, but because I actually enjoy their company and trying to arrange the conversation so that they will feel free to bring it up if they want to and ideally will feel sure that they're going to do so without my being judgemental. That they can say anything they like, however shocking it may seem. Then there may come a moment where a little chink will appear and I will feel that I can begin to approach them. Occasionally you meet somebody who's in such a state of either withdrawal or anger or resentment that nothing on earth will touch him, but that's the exception. Those people make it very clear to you. They'll be very honest in what they say. That's the one thing you can admire; they're not deceptive, they'll complain about everything and they'll probably tell you off because your attitudes are wrong.

What has been the philosophy behind your Homes? How, for example do you cope with setting up Homes in different cultures?

When Deng Pufang* gave his welcome speech to me there at the opening of our first Home in China, in 1989, he said, 'The reason we chose your Foundation is because you want to do it the Chinese way. Some international agencies want to do it their way and they seem to want to control us.' I can't believe it's true of all of them, but it's central to our thinking that we want each country to do it their way. In India, for example,

* Disabled son of Chinese leader Deng Xiaoping

there was wariness about our Homes at first because
the idea of sending one's relatives away to be looked
after was alien to the culture. But we were able to
project the Homes as just an extension of the extended
family, which they are intended to be, of course. You
get Westerners saying, 'Look at the standards in some
of the countries, they're dreadful,' but you have to say,
'That's their life – you can't impose St Thomas's*
standards on a Moroccan village.' It isn't the way they
think. I agree it's a lower standard, but we'll gradually
improve it. I'm an advocate of partnership between
state and private enterprise and seventy per cent of our
money for running the Homes in the United Kingdom
comes from the government. You need some government money to stimulate local people to find the balance. In the poor countries the local community finds
every penny – if we get the money from the governments of those countries, it's only taking it away from
another area of need.

*But a lot of people nowadays do argue that residential
homes are out of place in modern society – that they're
old-fashioned and institutional and that too much money
is spent on too few people...*

   Yes, a lot of agencies don't like my Foundation
and the residential homes. There's a newly formed
school of thought which argues that all disabled people
could and should live in their own homes. What is
required is to give them support, properly designed
living accommodation and aids and gadgets. Well this
community-based rehabilitation, or CBR, is excellent

* A London hospital

and we warmly support it and always have, but to say there is no place for the residential home is in our view a gross over-generalization doing a great disservice to disabled people.

I would claim that we were community-based from the very beginning, 35 years before the term was ever thought up. It was the local community which provided the money and the help; to me it was a matter of it taking responsibility for its own disabled. I'd further argue that the residential home is an essential step in the total rehabilitation process. For one thing, there are some people, particularly those with a progressive disability, who can never live in their own homes and may not want to. There are many who simply do not want the responsibility of organising their lives every day. If forced to, they can exist, but they can't live a meaningful life or have the same opportunity to lead a life of their own choosing that they'll get in a properly run residential home. Secondly, others who become disabled need a period of rehabilitation in the broad sense, not just the medical sense, to get to the point where they can go out into the community. You find that, even with those determined to move out, there's a two-year period coming to terms with disability and learning how to live with it. You see some disabled people have never done for themselves many of the ordinary things we take for granted; they've never budgetted, never bought and cooked their food, never organised the household chores. So we see our task as helping such a person get organised to the point where, with a care attendant's help, they can get an independent flat or bungalow. Without that base they'd never do it. Also, they probably wouldn't take that step unless they knew that they could come back if it didn't succeed. Obviously we have to wait till there's a free bed but we always guarantee to take them back. Our objective is first to give the disabled person security, make him feel, 'This is my home; I can live here as long as I want to and I can live the life of my own choosing – so long as I don't make life difficult for others. ' And then, as far as possible, we want to create conditions in which they can realise their full potential: take up a hobby, or, better still, some financially rewarding work, but all this with a family atmosphere to it. I know nothing can replace one's actual family, but at least we try. So I think, when people talk about residential homes, they're thinking of the old-style institution and applying that to us.

In that case, has this new enthusiasm for CBR actually caused you practical difficulties?

Many of the people who've evolved this doctrine are theoreticians who sit behind desks and get bright ideas – that doesn't mean that you throw everything that's been done before out of the window. But they're listened to by the universities and they're listened to now by many of the large funding agencies, some of which are beginning to refuse to fund the promotion of residential homes in the poor world. In fact, one aid agency which had been extremely nice to me when we were all together at the conference where I negotiated the deal with the Chinese and offered any advice they could give me on starting up in China, then went to the Chinese and said, 'Have nothing to do with Cheshire'.

But isn't it true that, if people are secure in a Home, they could get complacent? They haven't got the chance

to develop their independence and aren't challenged to
find out exactly what they can do on their own.

Well nothing that you produce is not going to have
snags, but I would say that there is a challenge, because
they're surrounded by people worse off than themselves who are doing more than they are. If they're
living in their own homes the danger is that they'll be
over-protected. We've had dozens of people come to us
from home – for a holiday in the first instance – who
say, 'for the first time in my life, I've been able to take a
decision or a risk. Because if I want to go across to the
store and buy some cigarettes, Mum will say, 'Oh no
dear, we'll come with you, much better, it'll be safer for
you'. She does it out of good intentions but it's not
what the person wants.

Sometimes disabled people are not over-protected
but actually unwanted. Family ties are strong in Ireland, but we had somebody in one of our Homes who
came for a holiday and when we took him back, his
mother said, 'What's he doing here? Take him away,
we don't want him.' The people at the Home were
really shocked and scrambled around and made a space
for him and he's as happy as anything now. And he'd
been living all those years, obviously knowing he wasn't
wanted, unable to do anything. You'd have thought
that, in that little village, a disabled son would be
looked after by his mother and father.

Yes, the disabled person could be totally independent but if the neighbours have nothing to do with
him and he can't get any friends – what then? Relationships come into it probably more than the physical
position he lives in. If you live in an urban area you're
more likely to get friends and sympathetic helpers than

in a village. But my answer is, don't generalise. What
we should do is provide maximum living options and
let each person choose what he wants.

*You've been in contact with so many different cultures
and faiths on your travels. Does the way they look after,
or just look on, the disabled have anything to teach the
West – or Christianity?*

There is no question at all that all cultures can
learn from each other. There is hardly a country I've
been to that I haven't seen something new and something inspiring. It's slowly taught me not to judge everything I see by the standards we are used to at home.
Religion is perhaps a different matter and I'm not sure
that I can answer properly. Hinduism has some very
elevating things to say about suffering and adversity in
its teaching: one cannot but look upon Sadhus* with
considerable respect. But I don't think I can recall a
Sadhu coming to a Home specifically to visit or comfort the disabled residents. What tends to happen is that
the Hindus within a Home will build their own little
shrine as a centre of worship. But of course, the individual Hindu layman will do a great deal for the disabled. The fact I started in India on just a hundred
pounds of my own money and there are now twenty-
four Homes entirely financed by them, is proof that
they care. Much derives from their family ties, and to
what extent Hinduism has a bearing on that, I'm not
qualified to say.

Perhaps I know less about the Muslims but I've
heard some very inspiring things from them. I remem-

* Hindu holy men

ber vividly in Poona, we started a little Home in a tent and later moved to a small house which had no kitchen, so I used to get the food from a cafe just a hundred yards away. One day, I found the owner had been seriously injured and had become paralysed. I said to him how sorry I was, and he thanked me and then added, 'But we must thank God whether we receive good things or bad things, for it is his will.' He was really in great trouble and distress and I found that most inspiring. He wasn't just repeating something he'd learned, he clearly meant it.

And what other lessons have you learned from the disabled?

I don't think you can repeat often enough that disability doesn't apply only to people who have a physical or mental handicap; it can be mental, physical or emotional. Somebody who's got a very difficult personality, who gets angry at the slightest thing, is disabled. All of us have got our personality defects that make us slightly unattractive socially, or bad employees or bad husbands, so I think we need to recognise that disability applies to all of us in one form or another. So the first thing we must not do is to put people into a category, 'the disabled,' as if they were different from us. Now I find that, if you live amongst disabled people, or if you become involved in their struggle to lift themselve above their limitations, you first see the way that they accept life with all the restrictions that their particular disability has imposed on them. A lot of them can never have a boyfriend or girlfriend, they can't have a career, they can't just decide to get up and do this, that or the other, they are dependent to a very large extent upon

other people doing things for them and yet they retain an
inner peace and a sense of purpose and a joy. I find that
extraordinary. The more you ponder it, the more extraordinary it is, because most of us get our peace and joy
from the external things we have – our position in life,
getting the car we want, and, if we lose them, we lose our
joy. So there's a big lesson to learn there. It's not a lesson
that's taught, it's a lesson you see being lived out in front
of you and you'd have to be a very shallow person to be
with disabled people for long and not think about that.

And the second thing is that, when you see somebody disabled, you have the feeling that you'd like to
do something to help. I don't mean in a sort of patronising, giving way, but by becoming involved in his difficulty and his desire to achieve greater independence.
That's pulling you out of your little world, and, that's
the one thing we need, to be pulled out of ourselves. It's
certainly true that the more we get involved with other
people's needs and hopes the more fulfilled we become. But then, at a spiritual level, we also need to
know that by ourselves we can do nothing. We depend
for everything on God. It may not appear so, but it's
true, and in this the disabled person, though he may not
have an actual faith, is better at realising his limitations
and his weakness. The trouble is that the more able we
are, the more intelligent, the more powerful and so on,
the less we think about our dependence on God. I
certainly find that, the more I feel in control of things,
the more I've learnt now, after these forty years, that
that is a dangerous way to feel. Uncertainty is far better
because it forces you to pray, though it's not so much
the praying as the inner disposition. And I find that it's
borne out in practice. When people join the committee
of a Home or come and help, they start with quite a

materialistic or worldly outlook and you see them gradually change. I think that, if God can't reach us through the Church or through our friends who've got a faith, he reaches us through suffering when we come close to people who suffer, or when we suffer ourselves. We do in fact find that we're much closer to God and the veil that hides him is much thinner.

There are other spiritual lessons too. Obviously with everything that you do in life, you need to know your ultimate goal, and with the disabled, people usually talk about independent living. Well, clearly, independence is only a relative term because we belong to a human family and for everything that we do we're dependent in one way or another on other people, so I think the best definition of the ultimate goal would be 'freedom', helping the disabled person become free to choose the way of life that he or she wants. It makes me think about freedom, which seems to me fundamental to man. We're told that God made man in his own image and that's a complicated concept, but, among other things, it means he's made us to be free because God and God alone is supremely free. There is a 'freedom from' which you might describe as a negative form of freedom. How far am I free from restraints imposed on me by other people, by the environment I live in, by my inner needs and requirements and equally my inner faults? If I've got a hot temper, then, to a certain extent, I'm a prisoner of that temper, if I have an inward disability or a physical disability, that's another restraint on my freedom. Also, relationships impose a certain restraint on me. So, except for God, there's no such thing as absolute 'freedom from', only a relative freedom. 'Freedom to' is the positive side – the freedom to do things, though of course you can be free to do something good or you can be equally free to do something bad. But there's also 'freedom for', and I think that freedom derives its real dignity and full dimension from the sense of being free for the service of other people. If I'm not free, then I'm not responsible for my own life but the freer I am, the more responsible I should be to assist the well-being of other people.

Politicians will speak most eloquently about the merits of freedom, but if you stand back and look at our Western world, can you really say it's such an ideal society? It has many excellent qualities and I go along completely with the call to join and build up the free world, but the freedom of our world is mostly used to enhance our own good. There is that phrase in the Bible 'Much is required from the person to whom much is given' (Luke 12:48). In a sense, freedom is part of love and if love isn't an outward giving love, it becomes stagnant, like water. Water remains fresh only so long as it flows.

We want the disabled person to be as free as possible from the handicap of his disability. Obviously we want him to use the freedom for a good purpose and we have a responsibility to try and help him see that, though we have no right to impose anything on him. And in the same way we want society to be free but we can't stop at that; we've got to work and see that people use that freedom for a good purpose. And very often, I'm sorry to say, we find that in the societies that are oppressed there is a stronger life of the spirit than there is in the free countries which have great material wealth. I remember well driving with my wife into Communist Poland years ago on Christmas Eve. We spent Christmas night at Lodz – and people were walking to Midnight Mass – some as far as twenty miles – from about nine o'clock onwards. In a western society people would demand transport, they would demand that the Church made things a bit easier for them.

And to go back to what you asked earlier about different cultures: I've noticed also that disabled people in poorer countries will put up with things that they'd never put up with in Britain or the United States. I'll never forget seeing paraplegics in a northern suburb of Barcelona, cheerfully wheeling themselves up a steep hill to get to the transport to their workshop. I've never seen a disabled person do that sort of thing as a matter of routine in Britain or the United States.

Then look at the Philippines. We've got eighteen Homes there and nearly all of them have no staff. The residents do their own washing, cooking and shopping. They even insist on working to raise the money to rent their building. We had our Far Eastern regional conference in Manila in the 1970s and Mrs Imelda Marcos came and opened it. She was very friendly and warm and said to me, 'I think this is wonderful, I will see that they get some financial help.' When I told the residents this, they said, she won't! We're not going to take one penny from Mrs Marcos!' And in that poorer community, there's much more willingness to help yourself in a a domestic sense. The disabled person in our UK Homes is hobbies in a remarkable way, but he wont't do domestic work. The spirit is the same, but here in Britain, the attitude would be, 'No the state pays for us, therefore we have a right to have our rooms cleaned.' That's not the fault of the individual; society's set that standard and so we take it as normal. But I do have to say that, in the countries that are oppressed and that are poor, there's a greater willingness to help the person in need than there is in a rich society.

5
Family

One day in 1955, when Cheshire and a small party of volunteers were trying to restore a large, derelict house, Ampthill, in Bedfordshire, he had a visitor who wanted his advice. Already a prominent charity worker herself, her name was Sue Ryder.

How strong was your urge to become a monk?

Oh it was very strong and I went to great lengths to explore it. When I first considered it, I'd stopped full-time work with the Homes because I thought, that, with the committee running things, I wouldn't need to be there. So as I had been after the war, I was disorientated. Solesmes was my first ever visit to a monastery. I went there feeling frightfully serious and pious and thinking I had to be on my best behaviour and look devout, but I just couldn't get over their, well humanness, how normal and friendly and smiling they were. And then that contemplative life overwhelmed me, because these were people living according to completely different standards from the world. And they had different reasons to justify their life. For instance, I remember one of them saying, 'There have to be courtiers – people who spend their lives in the royal palace looking after the King.' The argument against the contemplative life is, 'Suppose everybody did it, what would happen?' Well that's an absolutely ridiculous statement. It's like me saying that it's a very good thing to be a pilot and somebody else saying, 'What if everybody was a pilot?' People would never say it about a different profession. The truth is, there's a multiplicity of jobs, a multiplicity of gifts and everyone should follow the one for them. I spent the whole of Lent and Holy Week at Solesmes, doing a retreat. I was toying with the idea that I should become a contemplative. That's persisted with me, that tension, well, almost till today.

I know you may think I come back too much to that analogy of the battle, but it seems to me so fundamental in the spiritual life that it's inescapable. It's at the heart of it all. The men of prayer were to me in the forefront of battle and I felt that's where I wanted to be. But then, while working down in Cornwall with Barnes Wallis on his swing-wing project, the epileptic boy came to me, which led to my second Home. Shortly after that, I was taken out of the running with TB. The advantage of that was that it put me in comparative solitude. I refused to have any newspapers. They wanted to put pictures up on my walls and I said I didn't want them. I studied scripture and theology – I mean I tried to, though it was beyond me! It was a time of retreat and prayer and I had the opportunity to read what the different monastic orders said about themselves. I looked for the monastery that I thought I should join, but you see, what was wrong, looking back, was that I was always searching for the most perfect monastery: the most secluded, the most austere. That's an indication that you're on the wrong line. Usually the true sign of a vocation is that you're being called from within but you resist it. I know one Carthusian monk who ended up by actually kneeling at the altar and shaking his fist at God: 'I will not!' But God won in the end.

Midhurst gave me the opportunity of standing back and thinking about it objectively and the day came – it's clearly imprinted on my mind: St Cecilia's Day, 22 November 1953 – when I absolutely knew that my career lay with the Homes. It was a similar kind of experience to finding the Faith and finding the Church. But I still wanted to spend time in a monastery and, in the course of reading about the monastic life, stumbled across the Carthusians who lead the most solitary life of all. I wrote to Parkminster, the one Charterhouse in England, and I got such a friendly answer that I asked whether, on my discharge from Midhurst, I could go straight to them for a week's retreat before getting back to work. That was the second time the monastic life made a deep impression on me. There was a far greater solitude, a deeper solitude, a much harder life than the Benedictines, but the same friendliness and humour and, I have to say, remarkable understanding of the human problems of those who live in the world.

Four years later, when the Homes here and abroad were organized on a basis that ensured their future, I thought, 'Yes I can serve them better by withdrawing, becoming a monk and spending my time praying for the good of the world and them in particular.' So I appointed somebody to take my place and thought, 'Now I'll disappear.' But when I applied my mind to it in the concrete, I began to have doubts. Was I evading my responsibility? The first time I approached a monastery, I had been asked, 'What responsibilities do you have to your family or to others? Are any of these incompatible with your coming here?' The memory of that fetched me up short. Then we got married and I gradually began to think, 'Well there must be a way of combining the two. They aren't necessarily in contradiction', and so, in fits and starts with a lot of marking time, I think that's what I've been looking for, a way in which a part of my time is spent in the quiet of contemplation and the rest fiercely engaged in action. I'm still looking, hoping that, step by step, I may get there.

You said that belief in God would put restrictions on you. Was one of the reasons why you wanted to become a monk to escape from female company. Did you see girls as some sort of temptation?

No, I don't think that was a problem for me at that time. Yes, I'm attracted towards attractive people; it's only human. But after I became a Catholic, that side wasn't really a problem for me. It was before; it wasn't after. Mgr Vernon Johnson said to me one day, 'It seems extraordinary that you don't seem to be bothered by being in the presence of attractive women.' It rather surprised me, I suppose because I was in my initial fervour and that carries you along. I can't believe that there is anyone who can truthfully say he hasn't had difficulties at times and had to struggle, but I think that God, who knows my weaknesses, has protected and helped me. The trouble is, we fail to be grateful enough to God for what he does or saves us from. 'What does it profit a man to gain the whole world but lose his soul?'

What part did your marriage to Sue Ryder play in your faith 'journey'? You resisted it at first, didn't you? But do you now see it as part of God's plan for you?

Very definitely I do. From that cold February day when she came over to Ampthill, I felt there was something to be done together. But marriage never occurred to us. The Homes were my work and marriage clearly had no part in it. Anyway so I had kept telling myself. Perhaps I was a bit complacent there. Looking at people enjoying their family lives, I used to say that, given my circumstances and my objectives, I was fortunate that my life was organised so that I could give all my time to my work and religion. During that little interlude in 1949-50 when I thought it was the end of my time with my Homes and I would get back to a normal life, I nearly got engaged, to a French girl, but once I'd given that up, I said to myself, 'This is my work,' and kept telling myself that marriage had no part in it.

So what changed all that?

You know how it is in life, if you meet someone whom you feel totally attracted to, especially if you find that you share the same values and objectives. Even so, the thought of marriage didn't enter my head nor Sue's for nearly four years; the conviction that it was incompatible with my work was too firmly entrenched. But in the end the attraction proved the stronger.

Tell me something about Sue Ryder.

As a young girl, she had joined Special Operations Executive, who parachuted agents behind enemy lines, and had been attached to the Polish Section, one of her principal jobs being to drive the agents out to the aircraft, check that they had no identity give away on them and that they knew their brief. Her admiration for the way the Poles had fought, while at the end of it not getting the freedom we had promised them, decided her to devote the rest of her life working for them. She had gone into Europe in the wake of the Allied advance, seen concentration camps and set about helping the survivors and others of all age groups, then confined to hospitals and repatriation camps – a formidable task. When Germany was given her sovereignty back, the major aid agencies pulled out, leaving the Germans to take over. But Sue stayed on. She knew that the memory of their terrible suffering was too fresh in the victims' minds for them to be willing to go to the Germans with their problems. She came to Ampthill because she was looking for ideas on how to set up a new aid organisation. In her I saw a kindred spirit, doing the same kind of work but in a different way and so we used to exchange ideas and help each other. And then the time came when I felt compelled to put the question. Happily, after a little delay, she answered yes. As I rather feared might be the case, the priests whom I knew were by and large not in favour. They felt that marriage was incompatible with the work I was doing and so thought I was losing my vocation and in a way letting the side down. They thought that I was living more or less like a monk in the world and what did that have to do with marriage? I have to confess that this threw me a little on the defensive and for a short while genuinely worried me. Mother Teresa, however, thought the opposite. She was genuinely pleased and looked upon it as a gift from God to each of us for the benefit of our respective work.

What I can say now is that marriage was my saving. It stopped me taking myself too seriously. For one thing, if you do the kind of work I have been doing, too many people start saying how wonderful they think it is or how much they admire you. I don't think it is wonderful at all, anyway not in the sense that they mean, but the danger is that some of it will rub off on you and, without realising it, you will get self-satisfied and think you're someone important. Out and about, you can put up a façade, give an impression that you're a lot better a person than you actually are. In marriage, you can't possibly keep that up, your real self reveals itself; to be brought down a peg or two may not be what we like, but it's what we all need, and, vice versa, what we owe to those we love.

The other danger is that I had been too free, free to follow my own whim, free to go where I wanted. India made such an impression on me and the needs there were so great, that I began to think that this was where I

should set up my base. I remember arguing this out
with Father and Mother, telling them, 'You know there's
really nothing to pull me back to England.' Not only
was this rather a horrible thing to say to Father and
Mother, it revealed the lack of objectivity and logic in
my reasoning. The United Kingdom was where it had
all started, where I had built up my base, appointed a
Board of Trustees and legally delegated to them full
authority to run the UK Homes. To build a second base
in India and to be in charge of it would give a new
freedom, but it would split the Foundation. Once I was
married, it was different. I had a tie. I couldn't just do
whatever came to my mind, anyway not major things.
If you're living inside an Order or Community you
have an anchor; I had the framework of my Homes, but
it was not at all the same thing; I was too much my own
master. So I think that, as well as the positive side, the
mutual fulfilment and joy that we have each derived –
more and more as the years go by – marriage kept my
feet on the ground, it kept me more balanced. You do,
of course, have problems, for instance the difficulty of
how much time to give to your children and how much
to work. I don't know how well we solved it.

And we both had the same objectives. I mean my
idea of a honeymoon was to go and start another Home
together. It also happened at a time when I wanted to
found a Home in India over which I and not the local
committees had control. I was thinking how to do this
and then wishing, 'If I could just have a partner.' So we
founded Raphael together. It all fitted.

Obviously I get great inspiration from Sue. I see
somebody always willing to put herself second to what
she sees as the good of the work. She may, in my
opinion, overwork, she may take on things it would be

better to leave to somebody else, but she only does so
because she cares so deeply and has so total a dedication and commitment. I don't often detect the little
calculation of self-interest that tends to come into too
many of our decisions, too many of mine, certainly.

Do you now see marriage as another form of vocation?

Yes, I start from the premise that everything is a
vocation, whether you're a sweeper or a writer or a
Prime Minister or a priest, there can't be anybody whom
God doesn't call to play his or her part in the wonderful
work of completing his creation. But marriage has got
its special difficulties, its special opportunities, its special joys. I mean, marriage does call for an unselfish
love, doesn't it? And the marriages that break down are
probably those where you love that person for what you
think they are going to give you. However much two
people are attracted to each other, there are bound to be
difficulties and conflicting interests. It may be that I
come back tired and want an early night and a rest, but
my wife comes back with a lot on her plate, or a stack
of telephone calls to make, and the other way round.

The wonder of God's love is that it's totally, continually outward-looking to an extent and in a way that
is as far beyond our power to imagine as East is from
West. But our love is not like that, ours is an admixture
of selfishness and genuine love, the former usually
outweighing the latter. The thing is, we live in time and
space, we're finite and therefore think in little compart-
ments, so the all-embracing statement, 'God is love',
has to be broken down into its component parts and
quite closely defined, if we are to know what we're
talking about. If the Christian calling is love, then,

whatever state of life we find ourselves in, we are called to exercise love, and it's got to be a self-giving love, where you're willing to give the whole of yourself. The opposite is an inward-looking love and that's a terrible thing. If we could really see inside a person who was totally self-centred, I think we'd be absolutely appalled, because an inward love, locked up in itself, has no interest whatsoever in the good of other people only in what it can get out of them. So that's one sense in which I would say that marriage is a vocation. Vocation means a calling by God and whatever the actual form, it's ultimately a calling to love. We learn to love the God whom we cannot see, by loving our neighbour whom we can see. In marriage, we live a shared love, a shared freedom, and this helps, if not actually compels us to deepen our love and make it more outward-giving at the most personal level of our life. A man can give himself wholly to the service of the sick or the poor but, in his private life, remain far more self-centred than anyone would guess. In family life, that comes out into the open. One is challenged in a way that I don't think happens when one is on one's own.

What about the contrasts between your two marriages? The first, to Constance Binney, was before you had your Christian faith. Did that mean you had less of a sense of commitment?

I have to be honest and say that, in my first marriage, I had no thought of commitment. Marriage was something you could get into and then get out of if it didn't work. I don't mean that's how I really saw it; like I'm sure every young person, I used to dream every now and then of a beautiful, happy, exciting life-long marriage of love. But I was suddenly uprooted from my home ground. The Squadron had been suspended from operational flying for two months because of technical problems with the new four engine Halifaxes and as the end was not in sight, two of us were detailed to go to Canada and ferry back a Hudson. We drew straws and mine came up. I went home to collect some civilian clothes and remember walking across the field to catch the bus for Oxford en route for Bristol, from where the ship was to sail, and shouting out to Mother and Father, 'I'll come back married!' What on earth prompted me to say it, heaven knows, for I only expected to be in Canada a few days before collecting the plane. Probably an act of defiance; the two months marking time had got on my nerves.

On arrival at Montreal, I found technical problems there too and was put on what amounted to indefinite standby. It made me feel caged in. New York, I thought, the city of bright lights, jazz and Big Bands, only a few hours train journey away. I set off without permission, talked my way through immigration and four weeks' later was married. I'm not trying to excuse myself; there is no excuse. But I think you'll find that, in the war, people who were well under control and balanced at home, when posted, say to Los Angeles, quite often began to behave completely irresponsibly. For the first time in their lives they were virtually on their own, away from the structure within which they had lived and in a land of glamour and plenty.

No, I wouldn't have plunged into marriage in England with familiar faces around me and totally locked into the daily demands of the Squadron. As it was, I had an uncomfortable feeling in my heart that it was the wrong thing, that an eighteen-year difference in our ages would lead to future problems. But the future didn't count for much in those days and I was living in a kind of dreamland. Only as the war approached its end and I began to feel drawn towards something that I couldn't identify but which I knew would take me away from America where Constance belonged, did we face the inevitable and agree to part. If you ask me which of us was hurt or who had regrets, I don't think I can answer honestly. Whether rightly or wrongly, it is an episode I have long pushed into the past.

Now you mentioned that you'd had difficulties in balancing your career and your work with your duties to your family...

It gets difficult if you're being pulled in different directions. You've somehow got to organise your life so that, as far as possible, you have the different calls upon you in coherent order to enable you to move purposefully and calmly in one direction. Otherwise you'll end up in a mess. I know that that's easy to talk about as an objective, but by no means easy in practice, yet you've got to make it your aim. If you're in a state of tension, saying to yourself, 'I shouldn't be going to this function because Gigi wants to see me,' it doesn't work. You have to try and be clear in your mind, moment by moment, which of the calls on your time or your attention you should give priority to. That applies to the whole of life, but in family life it becomes more personal, more concentrated.

Did you feel, then, that you should have spent more time with your children, that you even, in a way, neglected them?

I wish I could have spent more. Those were lovely years and having to go away so often was a great wrench, for them too, I suspect. But as for neglecting, it depends what you mean. Really neglecting, no, but at times probably yes. I've got to say that, if the call came through now, I'd take off tonight without hesitation to go to Moscow to settle a deal for my Memorial Fund, but I ask myself, 'Would I do quite the same for Jeromy?' So it's not easy. I wouldn't say I'd got it right. But we've got lovely relationships – there's nothing wrong with the relationship.

How did you bring your children up as Catholics?

I'm not sure how well. I may have presented things in too grown-up a way or they may have thought I was over-pious. They don't quite share our views now. But in those days their faith seemed to sit so naturally on them, it was fresh and questioning and more than once had me wrong-footed. For the first ten years or so, they shared a room and that was where we all said night prayers together. One day Jeromy wasn't well, so we said, 'You can say your prayers in bed, Jeromy.' Gigi said, 'I want to say my prayers in bed too!' I said, 'You can't.'

'Why not? Is God everywhere but not in my bed?'

My technique when I wasn't too sure how to answer was to tell them to shut up, or just get on with it. So her question went unanswered.

After having foregone something he would dearly have liked to do, Jeromy asked, 'Dad, will that make the Devil sad?' I couldn't answer it, because I frankly don't know if the Devil is capable of being sad or not. Children have a lot to teach us. Caught in a dreadful

traffic jam on our way to a week's holiday, Jeromy saw
me getting fussed and impatient and rounded on me,
saying, 'Dad! You shouldn't be getting upset like that!
You should thank God that something worse hasn't
happened to us! All sorts of things could have happened to us – you should be pleased, not annoyed!' I
couldn't answer him, could I?

But I don't think we were very good at teaching
them to pray. I think we tended to rely too much on set
prayers. Perhaps it's more difficult – though it shouldn't
be – talking about it to somebody close to you. I think
perhaps I have failed in that. You can tend to be too
devoted to your faith so the other person thinks you're
overdoing it and puts his defences up. I admire the
people that are just completely natural with it, like
Mother Teresa – but I would think she has an effect on
everybody, wouldn't you? But you can't really attribute
causes to things can you? I mean we do, but we're more
often than not wrong.

How about material things? Did you indulge them?

Not really. We didn't have the money and they, on
their side, never wanted much. In fact, looking back, I
marvel at how little they asked for. Jeromy's favourite
Bible story was 'The Rich Fool'; I can still see him
with the little illustrated booklet in his hands, hooting
with laughter at the stupidity of a man putting all his
trust in money – and, in this respect, I don't think either
of them have changed.

*Do you, I wonder, see your family as a role model –
living in a community, sharing with people? Families
are often little nuclear units, very caring about each*

*other but not thinking much about people outside,
whereas your family is different – was it possibly of
benefit that you all lived in this way?*

I don't think it was particularly of benefit to Jeromy
and Gigi, no. But it was the only thing we could do,
given our circumstances. If I look back on my young
life, I had such a nice, secure, happy home, lots of
friends, lots of opportunities for entertainment and so
on. It was a bit different for Jeromy and Gigi; it's not
easy to entertain friends in this building. Well, I suppose there were things that counterbalanced it. We
could take them on world tours and they saw things that
they wouldn't otherwise. And they grew up learning to
take disabled people just as ordinary people.

*What about other influences in your life? Tell me about
Mother Teresa – she's obviously been very important;
she's helped your spiritual life, encouraged your marriage, given you ideas for your Homes. You often mention her as the person who leads the most perfect Christian life.*

When I went to India, I only had a capital of £100,
so I was fairly vulnerable and when I landed in Calcutta
somebody at the airport – I don't know how they got to
know about me, but I suppose there must have been a
tiny bit in the paper – came up and gave me 101 rupees.
The Indians never give you 100, it's polite to give you
101. That was about £6. So when I got my first little
committee meeting together, a few business people,
mostly British, I announced this, thinking it was marvellous. And the senior businessman said to me, 'Is that
all the money we've got?' and I said, 'Yes, but we

haven't started yet,' and he said, 'In that case I'm walking out. If that's the kind of rotten show you're asking us to contribute to, I'm having nothing more to do with it,' and out he stormed. And then I met Mother Teresa. You see, to her, money is nothing. She calls it rubbish. 'Throw it in the rubbish bin!' She was the first person I met who was certain that, if there is something to be done, you should do it and by one means or another God will provide. She doesn't mean you should sit back and just let him provide, you've got to work as if he's not going to provide, but you'll find it does come right.

She's got an enormous sense of humour. You know what got her going, don't you? She left Loretto and was under some suspicion, as you were in those days if you were a nun and left a convent, and set about learning some rudimentary nursing. She was walking past the hospital one day and she saw a body in the dustbin, and she looked at it and saw it wasn't actually dead although there were insects crawling all over it. So she lifted it out and carried it to the hospital. The hospital wouldn't take it so she determined to start up her own place. She set it up in Kalighat – that's the temple to the goddess of Death. And a little while later four or five members of an extreme Hindu sect came in and said, 'If you're not out of here by tomorrow we'll come back and we'll kill you,' and she said, 'Well why don't you do that now? Why wait till tomorrow? If you kill me now you'll just send me straight to heaven! Go on, do it!' Of course they backed off at that and never went back! But they went to the government and complained about her. The government came to have a look and were so impressed by what she was doing that they gave her full support.

The last time I saw her was a lovely experience. I was going through Calcutta two years ago in Holy Week and I wondered how I was going to manage to see her. Then, to my surprise, when I landed at Calcutta airport, I saw two of her Sisters sitting there. So I went up to them and said, 'Excuse me, Sisters, my name's Leonard Cheshire. I want to see Mother Teresa while I'm here. How do you think I could arrange it?' And they said, 'Well, if you just wait two or three minutes, she's going to appear. We're waiting for her.' And suddenly, through the door at the other end of the airport, in comes little Mother Teresa. And we had a lovely time together. I went to her Maundy Thursday service and after that we had a twenty minute discussion. I put a suggestion to her. That if you're praying silently and you suddenly get a wonderful, holy thought, you should not follow it, because, no matter how holy the thought is, it's infinitely lower than God. It can lead you miles away from what you started to do. And Mother Teresa thought for a moment and said, 'Yes, Satan can transform himself into an Angel of Light.' In her view, that was the way that Satan would use to divert you from a prayer that he knows is harmful to him.

On the way out to the airport to go to Bangkok, we suddenly passed little Mother Teresa's van trundling out somewhere, so I flagged her down. But as I did so, I could see her bent over with her rosary, praying. Just as she'd been at the Maundy Thursday service. I wish I could describe her at that service – she was squatting on the floor. She looked completely collapsed inside herself. That description probably means nothing to you but I think it was a bodily expression of the fact that her mind and all her faculties were just totally recollected inside, in communion with God, absolutely locked in prayer. I'd never seen a posture like that before. You see people praying rather beautifully but this was quite different. There isn't a minute when she isn't praying.

When the car stopped, she said, 'Come with me.' I said, 'Mother, I'm going off to a plane!' She tried to persuade me and then she said, 'Take my rosary!' Well I was so taken aback that I didn't like to take it, but then, when she'd gone, I thought what a stupid thing it was not to have accepted it so through a friend I got her a message: 'Did you really mean to give me the rosary – if so, please could I have it?' And a few months later, it turned up. I don't always carry it because it's bulky, but I usually keep it by my bedside.

When we were each building up our respective work she had suggested that we form an association between ourselves. And recently she said, 'That association never really worked, did it?' And I said, 'No it didn't Mother.' And she said,'Just as well, because we go about our things in a different way; we're associated in spirit but not in fact.' The sad thing is that she used to write me a lot of letters but then she told me one day, 'You're to destroy them all.' I said, 'Mother, why?' but she said, 'No you must destroy them' – it was a pity, wasn't it? I feel very close to her. During that little time we had together after the Maundy Thursday Mass she said, 'I pray two things for you: the first is that if God wants to take your Foundation away from you you won't resist' and I said yes – I can't see it happening but you never know, there must be something in it. And the second thing she said was, 'I pray that you'll have a long life but a good life.'

6
Suffering

'I look at the suffering in the world and I can't reconcile it with your belief.'

David Lean to Cheshire

*You are so closely involved with sick, disabled and
suffering people that you are probably in a better position than most to tackle a question to which it's always
difficult to get a satisfactory answer: Why does God,
who's a God of love and all-powerful, allow suffering?
How can it avoid shaking your faith?*

I was deeply affected by a book which described a
particular terrible moment on the first day of the Battle
of the Somme in 1916, when one of the soldiers shouted,
'Where's God in all this and if he's here, damn him!'
There's great pain in seeing somebody else suffering; it
runs completely contrary to our nature and what we
believe God to be and affects us so personally that we
cannot put it to one side as with other mysteries of the
Faith. So in that sense, it is the deepest of all mysteries.
I think that, as Christians, we shouldn't be satisfied
with saying, as we might with other mysteries of the
faith, that we can't penetrate it. We should at least do
our best to attempt a partial understanding of it. Given
the fact that suffering was the instrument God chose for
the redemption of the world, then it has to have some
profound significance.

I have thought long and hard about the problem of
suffering, and realise how little I still understand it, but
I can offer some personal thoughts. Can I begin by
looking at Creation? We know that God first created the
angel world, the world of spirit, then he created matter,
the material world. God created the universe for a purpose – to be transformed, and recreated in such a way as
to transcend its original nature and share his life in the
'New Heaven and New Earth' (Revelation 21:1). And
because he was the unifying factor for the two opposites,
matter and spirit, man, insignificant man, was given the

responsibility, authority and grace to be the instrument through whom this was to be achieved. Then things went wrong: first, we know from revelation that early in the creation process, a group of angels, led by Lucifer, rebelled and made a bid to usurp God's position. Here I am speculating, but it seems to me that they were told that man would have a higher place in the New Heaven and New Earth than they would and that was something Lucifer couldn't stomach: 'All those miserable little beings down there, you're not going to make them superior to us!' To my mind, the biggest mystery of suffering is not suffering itself but why those angels rebelled, since as spirits they were able to see the full consequences of all their actions, and then, why Adam rebelled as well. I do believe that, at some stage in the evolution of the earth, God picked out a man, Adam, and a woman, Eve, infused in them a spirit and gave them the ability to know him. It doesn't mean that the whole human race was descended from them. I think we can infer that Adam and Eve, whoever they were, walked hand in hand in intimacy with God, 'In the cool of the day' (Genesis 3:8). God, so to speak, made himself equal with them. He set limits on what they could lawfully do, but didn't pull rank. Then Adam and Eve rejected his instructions, taking the law into their own hands, taking upon themselves the right to decide what was morally right and what was morally wrong, usurping God's position. That's what's meant by eating the fruit of the Tree of Knowledge of Good and Evil (cf Genesis 3:1-14). That was the power and the viciousness of Satan's approach. He twisted God's words. I think that, in reality, Adam and Eve were probably faced with some sort of check-mate which, as they saw it, could be avoided only by ignoring the order not to eat the fruit.

But God did not use his divine power to over-
throw their decision. He wanted freely-given love. So
he was thrown out of his Creation. In his place the devil
was let in, like a virus, like the Fifth Column. What an
exchange! The more you actually sit back and think
about that original creation, the potential for good, the
beauty, the harmony, and then ponder on what Adam
and Eve did, the more you can see how really terrible
that original sin was. It's more than rebellion, it's absolute treachery, because God had more or less put himself into Adam's hands. But God decided not to repair
the damage from the outside, as it were coming in with
all guns blazing, but from the inside, where he's been
silently at work, putting things right, finally entering
human history in the person of his Son, who thus became truly man whilst remaining truly God. The result,
the price I think is the best way of putting it, was that he
was going to bear in his own human nature the full
consequences of what man did (Romans 5:12-21). So
Jesus bore every form of suffering in his own body, in
his own self, in his soul, and that is the extent of his
love for us (Isaiah 53:1-12). Having decided that, God
was entirely at our mercy, just in fact as he was with
Adam and Eve. Once you've accepted that first premise
and, granted, you can only accept it by faith, you can't
prove it by reason or science – the microscope can't
examine God – then everything else, it seems to me,
follows quite logically.

The one thing that's least understood today is sin.
How long ago it was that all this happened we have no
means of knowing. But, say it happened 40,000 years
ago, around about the time Homo Sapiens is thought to
have appeared, it means we've been accustomed for
40,000 years to a position where we've asserted our

own right to decide between what is morally right and morally wrong. In theory God could have taken away the authority he originally gave man, but, given his plan for man's role in Creation, he could not allow man's rejection of himself to allow the purpose of his creation to be defeated. That man still retained his authority is crucial to the question of suffering. And gradually, man's perception of God's goal for him grew dimmer and dimmer, and began to be replaced by man's own idea of what he wanted. Man was totally lost, like astronauts hurtling away into outer space with no means or power to come back. So you cannot hold God responsible for the suffering among men, nor, I hold, for the suffering that comes about through natural disaster. It was a result of his goodness, you might say, in giving us freedom. We are seeing a world that is partly the beautiful world that God created, but partly the distorted world that both the fallen angels and man have brought about. The angels undoubtedly have a role to play in regulating the cosmos (Psalms 91:10-12). To what extent the fallen angels have brought disorder into nature, no one can possibly tell, but it's a factor to be taken into account. The consequence of sin is death and suffering, so the result of Satan's success in winning us to his side against God's plan is a barrier of death and suffering between us and our arrival at the gates of heaven. We've all got to pass through it and take our share of it. If we can take a bigger share, it may mean a smaller share for somebody else. We should see suffering, not just as a trial we all have to undergo, but as an offence to God.

May I take an analogy from the disabled? Someone, for instance, who has a heart and mind like the rest of us, but who has cerebral palsy and can't move his arms in the way that a fully able and co-ordinated person can. Now I see in that disabled person a microcosm of the whole human family, organically one, just as the human body is, so that whatever affects one part of the body, like poverty, affects the rest of us as well. Suppose we had remained as we were originally intended to be, speaking the same language, united, totally fit and alert, using the maximum of our talents, all in co-ordination for nothing but the common goal which God had in mind, what the human family might have achieved and actually be today is bewildering, not least in harnessing the earth's resources to its good as well as ours. But sadly, we are a disabled human family, disabled by divisions, self-interest, injustice and so on.

Now, as I'm trying to say these words, the television screen is filled with the famine in Ethiopia. The same pictures, virtually, that we saw five years ago. Those terrible, overwhelming pictures, women and children, men and boys, sitting in a barren landscape with no possibility of food. When we look at that side by side with what we know about God, it's inevitable that it's going to cause us a major problem. But, when people ask how an all-powerful God of love can allow it, are they asking in good faith, or is it just a dismissive way of saying that God doesn't exist and there's no obligation to believe in him? If it's the latter, then it isn't really worth answering, because those people probably aren't looking for an answer anyway. Perhaps I've exaggerated there, but never mind. If on the other hand, the askers really want to know the answer, then I think they have to be warned, because they may well find themselves having to reassess their outlook, beliefs and way of life completely.

Instead of saying 'Where's God in all this?' ask

'Where am I in all this?' When we look at the famine in Ethiopia, it's self-evident that we, the human family, are major contributors to it. We've abused the environment and we've failed to address ourselves to a problem that's beset virtually every generation from the beginning of history. Then, there is in that country an oppressive government. Civil war is raging with obvious detriment to the aid programme. It isn't so much that the food is lacking – what is lacking is the means of getting it to the people. This is not something from which we can absolve ourselves; man's action is a major cause and we can't escape that and put the blame on God. The question we're addressing is, 'What responsibility has all mankind got for this disaster?' Farmers can certainly grow all the food that's needed for all the inhabitants of the earth. The only reason they don't is because those who buy are not prepared to put up enough money to pay for it. If the people in that part of Africa were my son, my daughter, I wouldn't let that happen. But the reality – and the first tragedy – is that we're broken down into little autonomous groups: individuals, families, communities, nations, each seeking their own end and each saying, 'What happens in other groups isn't my responsibility.' It's only when we begin to look at it in this light that we can grasp the real malice of sin. When there's injustice or poverty or an oppressive regime in some part of the world, it affects all of us. We can't just say, 'It's just Africa – let them run their own affairs and we'll get on with ours,' because we wouldn't treat an injured part of our body with that attitude.

All of us shy away from pain, but pain is an indicator of something wrong in the body. Have you ever stopped to think what would happen to us all if

pain were removed? If you broke your leg playing
football, you wouldn't know it and would go on playing. What then? Anyone who has worked amongst leprosy sufferers knows only too well. They lose all sensation in their hands and feet and can pick up a red-hot
saucepan and hold on to it not realising what is happening. That is why you see leprosy sufferers with stubs
instead of hands and feet. I go so far as to suggest that,
were it not for the warning signal that pain gives us, the
human race might not have survived, certainly not in its
present form. If that holds good at a purely human
level, then ought we not to consider its application to
the spiritual life? One can mount a strong case for
suggesting that much of the suffering we see in the
world may well be an indicator that something fundamental is wrong with us.

*Yet suffering so often hits innocent people. Those moth-
ers and children in Ethiopia didn't do anything to deserve their hunger. I still don't see why they're getting
it; surely they haven't sinned so grievously to merit it?
(Genesis 6:5; John 9:1-3)*

We can't escape from the reality that suffering is
going to overwhelm some people – the soldier in no-
man's-land in excruciating agony, the starving children
in some unknown part of Africa – and with the best will
in the world we can't alleviate it. But all I can say is
that suffering is our common enemy and you have to
look at it in the total unity of the human family. To say
that those children in the Ethiopian famine haven't
done anything to deserve their suffering is irrelevant.
They just happen to be somewhere where some disorder whose ultimate cause we can't identify, but is not

At the Oxford University Air Squadron Summer Camp, Tangmere 1938.

Leonard Cheshire with VC, DSO, DFC, S.E. Command, India 1944.
(Photo: Imperial War Museum)

Lord Wavell, Viceroy of India, (right) talking to Leonard Cheshire and Wing Commander Nicholson at the Viceregal Garden Party, New Delhi 1944. (Photo: Imperial War Museum)

Le Court, the first Cheshire Home, 1948-1954.

Arthur Dykes (right) in World War I. He was the first resident of Le Court. Leonard Cheshire nursed him until his death from cancer in 1948.

With Her Majesty Queen Elizabeth the Queen Mother at Le Court on the first Family Day, 20 April 1955. (Photo: Charles White)

With Gigi, Sue and Jeromy. (Photo: Richard A. Burne)

Leonard Cheshire with his wife Lady Ryder of Warsaw at Cavendish in 1975, when they received jointly the Variety Club Humanitarian Award. (Photo: Doug McKenzie)

Boetie playing chess with pointer, Port Elizabeth 1977. (Photo: Norman Potter)

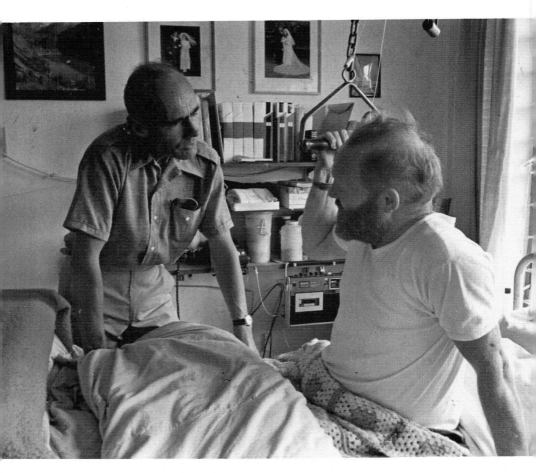

South African Tour, Queensboro 1977. (Photo: Norman Potter)

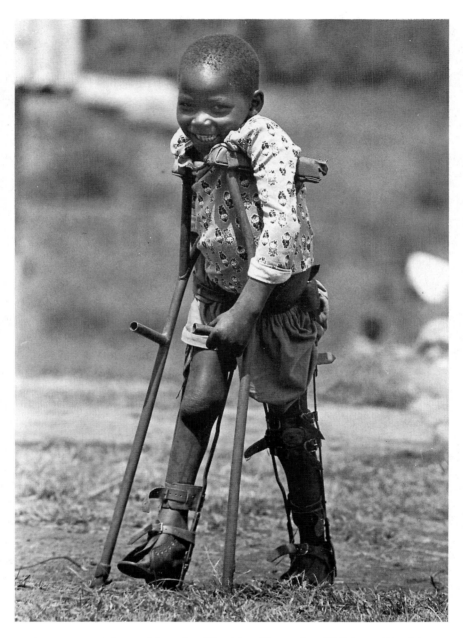

A young resident of Lusaka Cheshire Home for Children, Zambia.
(Photo: Norman Potter)

Her Majesty the Queen talking to a resident during the Cheshire Homes International Week, Tara Hotel, London 1981.

Leonard Cheshire on his 70th birthday with Peter Beadnall, a resident of Spofforth Hall Cheshire Home. They are holding one of the seven volumes containing signatures of residents, staff and helpers from Cheshire Homes worldwide. (Photo: Press Association Photos)

The Duchess of Kent re-opens the new wing at the Chiltern Cheshire Home, 12 June 1990. (Photo: Maria Bartha)

Leonard Cheshire with resident Malcolm Stewart on the 30th anniversary of Mayfield House Cheshire Home, Edinburgh, 1990. The occasion was made memorable by a visit from Her Majesty the Queen. (Photo: Scotsman Publications)

attributable to God, is now erupting. Jesus denied the Jewish idea that, if you suffered, it must be because you'd done something wrong. He said, 'Don't think that those people on whom the Tower of Siloam fell were greater sinners than others, they weren't' (Luke 13:4).

Yet although the suffering has come about, isn't it still possible for God to intervene in some way? Especially if, as you say, he's also deeply affected by it?

How do you suggest this would happen? Is God going to operate on a person's will and make him change his mind? If he does, then that person is not free to live out his life in his own way and either achieve his destined goal or not. Or, is it really rational to hold that God should, for instance, deflect bullets or manipulate a drunken driver's car so that it just misses people? That means nobody would know where they stood. There would be no predictability in anything and no direct relationship between what we do and its effect. God has to make us see that we are responsible for what we do and I simply cannot see how he can both do that and play around with the consequences of our action.

There's no denying the horror of suffering, but have you considered that God, in his own mysterious way, might already be limiting our cruelty? Now the evidence that God is a God of love is so universal that you can't dismiss it. How do you account for the consistency of belief throughout the Old and New Testaments? Witness after witness stands out in history from all walks of life, all races, willing to lay down his life, willing to sacrifice everything he's got in defence of God as a God of love. That is the primary reality in the light of which we have to examine the realities of our human condition.

There seems to be increasing discussion nowadays of putting an end to suffering through euthanasia. Just the other day, I heard that some parents were let off after helping their sick daughter to commit suicide. Some people would see it almost as a moral duty. Did you ever find that the dying people you sat with asked to die?

None of those I sat by ever said, or even hinted, at it, despite considerable suffering. I know that people in extreme agony do cry out, 'I want to die!' Wouldn't most of us? But are we, when under that pressure, the best judge of what's best for our future? We don't know what we're going to be like tomorrow.

What I do feel deeply, in our present age, is that the accent is on material prosperity and happiness. That means you've got a distorted view of the realities of life. Jesus said, 'If you want to be my disciples, pick up your cross and follow me' (Matthew 16:24). When he talked about the suffering he was going to undergo and Peter said, 'On no account is this going to happen to you' – remember? That was the one time that Jesus was fierce with Peter. He said, 'Depart from me, Satan!' (Matthew 16:23). He knew perfectly well that, only by going through it, could he accomplish the mission on which God the Father had sent him. Now your person who supports euthanasia would presumably have ended his life at that point. If you're saying that, whenever someone's suffering, they should be released from it by premature death, then you nullify Christ's vocation. You can't give up the Cross before the end – it's like giving up fighting in the thick of the battle. I'm convinced, though, that we do not have a duty to keep a man artificially alive when he's approaching death; that's quite different from arbitrarily cutting a life short.

I remember you saying that belief in God would bring responsibility as well as advantages. In a way it's easier not to believe, isn't it? You can see suffering and just say, 'Let's put an end to it'.

Yes, it's simpler. Yes, the powerful argument is that the way out is to kill the sufferer. And obviously you can't argue my way from the standpoint of someone who doesn't believe in the God of Christianity. If you say that life is nothing beyond this world, then of course the happier you are, the more you are relieved of burdens the better, but what are you left with at the end of it? The whole thing's just a waste of time. If all is going to lapse into nothingness, then why go through the struggle to build a better world? The man who doesn't believe will sooner or later find himself, if not in despair, at least frustrated, thinking, 'Was it worth it?' But if you believe that our real life is only going to start after death and that that life has a meaning and a fulfilment dependent upon and proportionate to what you've done in this life, then it must be different.

But God seems to be making it as difficult as possible for us to trust him. He does lead, but he also leaves us in a position where we can't see the road ahead or it looks as if it's totally blocked. But the more we are unable to see the road, the greater is the value of our trust in him, even though it seems to be in our worst interests. It's easy to love when everything's going right. But true love consists in loving when everything is going wrong. I believe, too, that the more a person suffers, the greater will be his capacity for joy in the world to come. Great mystery though it is, my understanding of God's revelation is that, by emptying yourself of ego, you make greater room for the power and the love of God to fill you in this world and correspondingly increase your happiness in the next. Happiness is an inadequate word: if we had even the most fleeting glimpse into what lies ahead I'm convinced that the horror of suffering as we now see it would look completely different.

That sounds like little immediate comfort to someone who's suffering.

I agree. I realise what I have said may affront, even scandalise. I would argue that, when somebody is suffering, you must not attempt to explain it. You must not attempt to preach to him; that is completely wrong. You must identify with him and do all in your power to comfort and relieve him. Preaching can come later. We all go through periods of our life when the problems we face are too much for us and we say, 'I want to get out of this.' And I believe that God almost likes it because it's a genuine cry from the heart. Jesus, too, felt totally abandoned yet he never lost faith. To many good Catholics, that cry, 'My God, my God, why have you forsaken me' – is a stumbling block. They feel affronted by it and go to great lengths to say he didn't mean it.

But to turn away from the wonder and joy of heaven because life's getting a bit difficult is not to our advantage. If someone sees his life as fruitless, look at him as part of a fighting unit – during the war, we had to encourage people and try to set them an example which would keep them going. The fact that he's in that state, means he's got something of the greatest importance to achieve and you're not doing him a service by diverting him from that purpose and saying, 'Yes, all right, fall out of the struggle.' I mean, heaven has to be stormed doesn't it? From the very word go, we have to struggle to keep alive, ask for our food if we're hungry, shout for our wants, struggle at school. You can put that another way and say that, for everything we want to acquire, whether a gift, a position in life, a skill, we have to pay a price and the price will be proportionate to what it is that we want to 'acquire'.

There was a close friend of mine at Oxford, Jack Randle. We both played rugby. I didn't like rugby, but there were only sixteen people at Merton who played, so, if one of them was ill, I used to have to play in the college team. Jack was like a young terrier. Once he got hold of the ball and ran, almost nothing would bring him down – one, two, three people on top of him but he'd somehow keep going – for far longer than you imagined he possibly could. The war came and he joined the Norfolks. He took part in the battle of Kohima.* Late one afternoon he was wounded, but he was in command of a small group and they were in a very bad predicament so he spent the whole of that night reconnoitring the position, deciding what he needed to do. When it dawn came, he led the charge against the Japanese position across a hundred and fifty yards, perhaps more, of open land. He hadn't gone very far when he realised there was a Japanese machine gun post on his left flank hidden in a pillbox. Unless that pillbox was silenced, he and his men would be finished.

* December 1944, during the Burma campaign against the Japanese

So Jack told the men to carry on, turned half round and charged the machine gun head on. The men who saw him reported that he was being hit as he charged, but he kept going right until he reached the pillbox, hurled a hand grenade into it and then finally just threw his body across the slit. For that he was given a posthumous VC. Jack Randle was one person who influenced me. He knew that everything hinged on silencing that machine gun. So first he had the ability to see what the top priority was and then he had the determination and the courage and the sheer will-power to make certain that he achieved his objective. Now all that he suffered as he charged and the loss of his life were the price that he paid for that little victory. So if we look at life in general, there are all sorts of goals that we seek, but there are some that are so precious to us that we would think nothing of giving everything we've got to achieve them. But if we look solely at the price, the suffering may well seem meaningless.

Again, the imagery of war plays a strong part in your thinking. But it may not be so easy for the suffering and those involved with them to identify with it.

No, but I'm completely convinced that it's true and that we need to recognise it. Our war is not really against other men but against spiritual evil in high places, against the powers of darkness – I know those are descriptive terms which are hard to understand. We tend to forget that there are angels who are in a state of total war against God's plan (Revelation 12:3-9) and war pervades every aspect of creation. And once you recognise the fact that you are at war, many things change, even the first superficial view of suffering. In war, suffering is not looked upon as something that's unjust, but something that's inevitable. And I think we ought to begin to see suffering in the world in that light. We know perfectly well that once there's a war there are going to be casualties, and in a war, when casualties come back from the battlefront, we surround them with honour.

Looking at another aspect of the argument. I heard a father on the radio this morning, discussing embryo experimentation. He said his nine-year-old son, who had just died, should not have been allowed to be born because of the extent of his handicaps. If embryo research had been possible then, the handicap could have been detected; some suffering could have been eradicated. Why do you believe it's permissible to allow a child into the world knowing it's going to be handicapped?

First, I refuse to accept that suffering is the worst evil. A person who, throughout his life, is going to hurt others because he just wants to achieve his selfish ends, is far more harmful to society than the boy who is born with a disability. Our final objective is to share the life of God; in order to do so, we have to be humble and recognise our dependence on God. Now the child who is born disabled may well be far more likely to lead that kind of life than the highly successful businessman.

This thinking that it's unfortunate to have a handicapped child as it's a burden on the family and so on, is something I genuinely sympathise with, but I have to say it's not far removed from Hitler's thinking. Hitler said, 'Look, we've got a Master Race, far better than the rest, why should we have inferior people on earth?

They can't advance the good of the world, they're holding us back, so let's eliminate them and re-people the world with our stock.' He included handicapped people with those to be eliminated, and the people who destroy embryos do exactly the same thing, except that they want to do it at an earlier stage than Hitler. They say, 'Oh we don't want suffering, so we can eliminate those who are suffering by ending their lives in the womb, and let people who don't suffer people the world.' But what sort of people are these going to be? Who has given us the authority to decide who will live and who won't?

I'm not judging. I know many people feel very deeply that the Church is bigoted and blinkered and object to the statement that the embryo is already potentially a human being. But if the scientist could see the embryo, not as something to be worked on, but as his son, with the personality he's going to acquire, and who suffers pain, perhaps even excruciating pain, while being killed, I don't believe he'd do it.

If people say it's cruel to let this child live, then they are arguing that a handicapped person can't live a worthwhile life and that's manifestly untrue. I've lived amongst disabled people for all these years and in my view, many of them lead much more meaningful and productive lives than a lot of able-bodied people. Previously, I'd judged a person's achievement by the achievement itself, wonderful if it was something spectacular, like becoming a Prime Minister or a pop star giving happiness to millions. But I now judge it by: 'What have I made of my opportunities and my resources?" The person with disabilities, no particular talents, no particular position, hardly enough money to live on, no friends, may well be the real achiever. Look at little

Boetie in that picture on the wall, playing chess with a
pointer on his head. Just with that gadget attached to his
head, he can make furniture out of half clothes pegs. He
can't use his arms except in jerks, but he's got strong
legs – he did a marathon in his wheelchair. Look at
Douglas Bader.* Before he lost his legs, he was just
another pilot, better than some, not as good as others,
but the loss of his legs somehow released an energy and
a spirit in him that would never have been released
otherwise. So he became a world figure that he would
never have been but for what you'd have called a
disaster. And look at Hilary Pole. She became totally
paralysed, only had movement in one toe, needed an
artificial breathing machine, artificial feeding, couldn't
talk, couldn't move. Wouldn't you have said, 'Let her
slip away'? But Hilary was absolutely determined to
live and not only to live but actually to make something
of her life – and look what she did! Through that one
big toe she learned to type and so to communicate. If
you expressed pity she'd give you a very sharp answer.
Then she started counselling other people with disabilities who hadn't come to terms with them. She could
say, 'Pull yourself together,' while I couldn't, being
able-bodied. She wrote some very moving poetry. Then
she launched an appeal to raise money to buy specialised equipment like hers for other disabled people and
ended up with getting the MBE.** I would say her life
was a greater life than some Prime Ministers' because
out of nothing, by worldly standards, she achieved all
this. Now that is a radical reassessment of achievement
and is linked to what I said about not being able to

* British wartime fighter pilot who had lost his legs in a pre-war flying
accident
** Member (of the Order) of the British Empire

judge courage without knowing the effort it's cost. I go
back to my point that we seem to have been created to
struggle and to reach forward and only by doing so do
we realise our full potential and so make ourselves
ready and fit for whatever lies ahead for us in Heaven
and that suffering and disability bring a maturity and
inner strength that an easy life doesn't.

*Hilary Pole was very seriously disabled but she did
have a good brain. Isn't it different when a child is so
mentally handicapped that it literally can't do anything
except be there?*

I don't think that's true. We have a number of
homes for mentally handicapped children and if you go
to one of them, you'd immediately notice that each has
got his own little personality, despite the fact that he
may grind his teeth, eat stones and so on, and the staff
have a great affection for him. You find that, given the
right routine and care, that little child can advance to a
position where he does things. At Raphael in India
we've got a very large mentally retarded unit, and the
first girl we had there, called Paiman, was picked up off
the streets. She had obviously been raped many times,
and she was wild, like a little lioness. She used to be
tied down but she always broke her bonds and she'd
climb over the eight foot wall and disappear. Then,
when we founded Raphael across the river in the lovely,
peaceful semi-jungle, she quietened down. She'd still
got a violent temper, but when I saw her last month she
was doing beautiful embroidery, she was smiling, and
she came up and gave me a squeeze, 'Would you take
me back to England?'

And in the picture by my desk on the wall, there

are two people acting on a stage, both mentally handicapped. In the photo, you can only see their backs. But
from the look on the faces of the audience – some of
them local V.I.Ps. – you can see that they're giving a
powerful performance. To me that's a beautiful photograph because it shows that people who you thought
had nothing to contribute could hold an audience.

And if you look at my life, it was changed first by
the war and secondly by disabled people. That gave me
a completely different perspective on life; it gave me
faith.

*You say that poor and suffering people can help the
able-bodied; again couldn't that argument seem rather
risky – in that it could make you complacent about
trying to prevent or alleviate disability, even by morally
permissible means?*

I think the point I'm making is that we all need
each other. When there's somebody who's suffering, in
whatever form, we feel moved to help them, but we
find, in doing that, that they have their own gifts which
they give back. They call us back to real values, to a
real sense of priorities. One of my crosses, in a way, is
people who say to me, 'How marvellous, you're helping these people!' Well I mean, what do you answer?
The truth is that people who work in any form of social
service are doing something for other people, but it
isn't a one-way giving, it's quite clearly a two-way
giving.

I was really locked up into trying to search for my
career, but when I met Arthur, I had to forget my career
and I had to think about him. He pulled me out of my
little castle and in doing that, he set me on the road to

becoming more fulfilled. I've already told you what
disabled people have taught me and time after time,
people have said, 'When I feel down and I feel life is a
waste of time I visit the Home and go back feeling it's
all different.'

*But have you ever suffered deeply yourself, for example
when you had TB?*

Yes, I was in pain, but not severe pain. I thought
I'd try and manage without pain relievers but found I
couldn't – I can still see the wry little smile on Matron's
face! I've been through little agonies of mind: 'Did I do
the right thing there, did I fail in this?' But no, I feel
I've lived a very privileged life. I've been through a
great deal of other people's suffering but I've been
pretty well untouched myself. I was never wounded in
the war - shot up and in difficulties, but never wounded.
Cold and occasionally exhaustion were about the worst
things. So I can't really bear much testimony on that
side but the day may come. But there were aspects of
the Midhurst experience I found a definite plus. For
example, when I had my two or three operations, one of
them quite major, I felt, in a way, completely relaxed,
totally in the hands of the surgeon and the anaesthetist.
That was quite a relief, because most of my life I'm
having to take decisions and activate things. It taught
me to accept what happened to me. That isn't to say
that I might not object in a different situation. And
another interesting thing: Geoffrey Todd, the famous
Australian TB doctor at Midhurst used to say that nuns
made worse patients than mothers of families. The nun
just lies on her back passively and says, 'I must accept
this,' while the mother says, 'I must get better quickly

to get back to my children.' Now there's something quite profound there: on the one hand we have to accept everything God gives with love but at the same time we have to fight suffering tooth and nail.

So what tactics would you use, given that you're also saying that we have to accept it?

There are two different but totally interrelated ways. The first one is to alleviate it – by immediate means, by giving food, or morphia, or companionship, and also to try and reduce and prevent and attack the causes. It's manifested in Jesus' life – he went about and laid hands and cured people (Matthew 9:35; Luke 6:19) – he saw suffering as something to be banished, overcome, reduced. But the second thing is we mustn't let suffering get the better of us, divert us from our goal, remain in close, loving, trusting union with God. Suffering is one instrument in Satan's hands which can destroy our faith in God, or stop other people coming to the faith.

I've met many survivors of the concentration camps over the years, through my wife's work, and I've quite often asked them, particularly the priests, what was the most difficult thing for them, and they always say, 'to forgive'. And suppose you look at Odette.* She was two years in solitary confinement and constantly brought out and tortured. I've known her for many years and we've always been friendly, but last year when we sat next to each other at tea, I said, for the first time, 'Odette, I'm simply incapable of picturing myself standing up to torture and not giving in.' And she said,

* Odette Sansom, captured and tortured for her role as a British agent in occupied France

'What a stupid thing to say! None of us know, but you'll find out when the moment comes it will be different; God will give you strength you never knew you had. The whole of the time, I stood at the foot of the Cross and said, "Lord, if you want me to be pushed beyond my endurance, all right, so be it, I shall have to give in, but if you don't want me to then support me." I looked on myself as a little miracle. I thought, "Here I am, just an ordinary little girl, and here are these people doing their utmost to get something out of me and they can't." That's not my strength, but it's happening to me.'

'My most difficult thing was to forgive. I just knew that I must not allow myself to bear resentment against them. If I did that, then I would have gone down to the same level as them; they could break my body, but not my spirit if I remain firm and trusted in God. Then I employed all sorts of little tricks. I was determined that when they led me away to be executed I'd look smart, so each day I twisted my skirt round a tiny bit so it wouldn't be worn out in one place, I found a piece of wood which I used to polish the floor, and so I took these little steps to keep my self-respect. One day, when they were getting ready to try and force some information out of me, they made a crucial mistake. They moved the chair to the window and I saw the trees and I said to myself, 'Well if this is the moment when I'm going to go I shall go to my end with the picture of those beautiful trees in my mind.'

Now, clearly she was in the front line of the battle against the forces of evil, and was determined not to be defeated by them but had she gone through life just with the normal ups and downs I don't think that thought would have occurred to her. And also – which surprised me, because I had no idea she had a religion – it made her realise her total dependence on God. She said, 'He's got me in his arms' (Isaiah 43:2-3; 49:15-16). I don't think we should ask for suffering, but if it comes our way we should know this is an opportunity of sharing in the redemptive work of the Cross and that it's going to advance the good of the world as a whole and diminish the power of Satan.

I think you can say that suffering is like a heavenly seed – by not being overcome by it, by not being turned into resentful, angry people, not losing our faith, or, if we do lose it, by regaining it again, we can make it flower in heaven. I know it's hard to understand; if you hadn't seen the process, you could never look at a funny little seed and say, 'One day it's going to be a beautiful flower.' But every minute of our lives is precious and every minute can be turned to good account, no matter what our condition, whether it's Hilary Pole, or the world's fittest athlete.

7
Prayer

In 1984, Leonard Cheshire went to Japan to make a television programme about the 40th anniversary of the Nagasaki atom bomb. Newspaper reports made much of the fact that Cheshire, excluded from the annual official commemoration ceremony, went instead to a church and spent the time quietly praying.

A lot of people find prayer difficult. Yet it seems so much part and parcel of your life and you've spoken of its great attraction. How would you advise someone to approach it?

My problem as I'm speaking to you, is to pull my mind back from the hectic weekend conference and all the things I had to get set in motion this morning, some of which aren't quite finished. But I find myself in the course of the day gradually turning to prayer. It seems to me that prayer is a journey, a lifelong journey, a journey that goes by fits and starts. There are times when you move quickly along the road; there are other times when you don't move at all. And there are times when you get attracted by something off the road and forget that you are on a journey. It's a journey with a destination and I would define that destination as mystical union with God (Exodus 6:8; Hosea 11:1-4; Psalms 116:6-8). But it's not a lone journey; it's one you do with a companion. You're walking side by side with God, and, as you start the journey, you're more or less unaware of who he is. The more you progress along the journey, the better you know him. But he is both your companion and your end, so it's unlike a human journey, and at any moment in your life, your prayer sums up the totality of your relationship with God over the past five years, or fifty years, or whatever it is.

No one thing you can say about prayer totally describes it. We're called throughout the New Testament not just to pray but continually to pray and I find those quotations striking and challenging. 'Stay awake, praying at all times for the strength to survive all that's going to happen,' in Luke (21:36), for example.

But you lead such a full life – how on earth do you find the time to pray?

The way I've been slowly working it out is that you first make a rule that you're going to say so many prayers in the day. It may be few or it may be many but you definitely set your times and adjust them according to each day's different circumstances. Obviously you get days when you simply can't find the time to set all those periods aside and for instance, yesterday I had a busy day but I had a period when I was at lunch with people. And when they were talking amongst themselves, not to me, I slightly withdrew from the conversation and went through my intercessory prayers, just saying the odd thing and hoping people didn't think I was being rude but with enough of my mind on what was going on to re-enter the conversation at the appropriate moment. But talking to the real men and women of prayer who are really praying most of the day I find that they're doing it in such a way that you wouldn't know it. I think that it is perfectly possible to be completely absorbed in another person's conversation and yet be praying in your heart. It can also make that conversation more meaningful. I say 'heart', because you can't make that sort of prayer with the mind – it would be split. But if you're deeply in love with somebody, then no matter what you're doing, down in your heart your inner desires turn towards that person, don't they? That will never leave you. So the prayer of desire should never leave you, although you may have no room in your mind at that time to turn to God and, at odd little moments between conversations, you find that your spirit, not your mind, will rise in prayer. And when you do get a minute to go and fetch a cup of tea or something, then you'll find that you do say a little prayer, where the mind comes in as well as the heart. All of us stumble when we start, but I'm convinced that that is what the call to pray all the time basically means. Yesterday I didn't find the time to finish all my prayers, so I tried to fall asleep praying. Mother Teresa convinces me. Every time she's not having to talk to somebody she is praying and praying deeply and so I'm convinced that when she's actually talking to you she's talking absolutely naturally and with a lovely beautiful smile but prayerfully.

I aim to set aside forty-five minutes a day, morning and evening, for silent prayer, – what the Desert Fathers called the Prayer of the Heart. I go to Mass each day if it's possible, but if it isn't, I try to read it privately. If I can't get hold of a Missal I just go through it in my mind. I say the Office each day and after lunch, if possible, I set forty minutes aside for intercessory prayer – for the Homes and for people. I pray the Rosary – not everyone likes the Rosary, but I think most people do. It depends how you say it. I find it extremely useful when you say a devotional prayer, like each decade of the Rosary, to do it for a specific intention, for somebody that you want to pray for or anything that's important to you at the moment. Then you'll think, 'If I don't give my full attention to what I'm praying, I'm letting them down.' I often find it makes me go back and restart. Distractions do come; you can't help them, like noises outside the window. But you can stop concentrating on them. Just let them float through your mind.

Some days when I'm travelling it becomes a bit difficult to fit the timing in. I can get periods on the plane and make up for it then. The trouble is, you can get mentally tired so that you can't actually settle your mind down. Where I know I've failed, and I won't say it's the only place, is in not taking the opportunities between the ordinary events of the day.

So what's the best way to start praying?

Whatever way comes most naturally – the Our Father, asking for something you need, starting and ending the day with just a few moments of prayer. But you need to move forward. I find the foundation of my prayers in the Divine Office, the Breviary, because you're praying the prayer of Christ with him and you're learning the Church's way of praying. It's perhaps the best introduction to serious prayer, though you can't put the Office above the Mass of course, because the Mass is the Sacrifice of Calvary.

And what do you think is the most important prayer?

At the beginning, it should be the simple prayer of asking. Because when you start, I mean whether it comes to you late in life, like me, or whether it comes to you as a little child, you start by asking, as it's the only prayer you know and God likes us to ask. I remember going down a beach in Portugal with the family, and Jeromy at that time was very young and frightened of fierce-looking dogs. And he was walking along this little ledge, only wide enough for one person, when suddenly in front of him was a huge and rather menacing-looking dog. Normally he would have shrieked but this time he didn't – he immediately asked God for help, absolutely spontaneously and naturally in his tiny little way, I can't remember exactly what happened next; the dog was friendly, they just passed each other or the dog turned round and went back, but it was just one of those lovely instances of a little child whose first thought was, perfectly simply 'Please help.' It isn't that God doesn't know what we want, but to ask is to express our recognition that he's our Father and that we expect him to answer. So we mustn't try and make it complicated or use clever words; it's just a simple request from the heart, and I think the shorter the prayer, consistent with what you're saying, the better. Every prayer has to be proportioned to its purpose. If you're in the military or the police, you are taught economy and precision of words. And that is one of the means by which the armed forces and the security forces are efficient and can act promptly. I suggest it's got something to teach us about prayer.

Three years ago, I was in Auckland, New Zealand, staying in a friend's house. We were sitting downstairs and I heard some popping upstairs that sounded a bit peculiar. Something in me kept half telling me to go up and have a look. There's a lesson there, those little inner voices that niggle at us. Then something happened that made me go up and fetch something and I saw to my shock that the mattress was on fire and the fire was already beginning to blacken the walls, which were wooden. Now I had to act very fast but I couldn't decide which was the greater priority. Move the bed? Get some water? If so, in what? Look for the fire extinguisher? Then, realising I couldn't cope, I shouted out just three words: 'Bucket of water!' People came running upstairs and together we threw the mattress out of the window and put the fire out. When everything had calmed down, I asked John what he'd thought when he heard, 'Bucket of water!' He said, 'The way you said it told me what to do'. I've heard Sue say: 'I ask you, God, to do with me what you want.' In itself one of the purest prayers you could make. But it was the way she said it that arrested me, and moved me.

But we're talking about the beginning, aren't we? You begin with asking, but then you gradually get taught that, in addition to asking, you've got to express sorrow. You've got to express your dependence on God, you've got to praise him and above all say 'Thank you'. I think that's our greatest shortcoming – we ask but we don't say thank you. And that seems to mean a lot to God, because in the story of the Ten Lepers, Jesus immediately said, 'Did only one come back and say thank you?' (Luke 17:11-19) The more you ask the better, so long as you balance it with a thank you and so long as you don't lose faith because it seems you aren't answered.

I think we have to understand that we can't pray properly on our own. We've got to recognise that it's God who prays in us, and that is, I think, a kind of inversion of today's values. Today's priority is action; there are so many needs in the world that even very holy priests say we should be up and doing all the time. A priest, far more spiritual than I, once told me, 'All day I'm responding to needs; I don't have three minutes to spare.' So when you confront them with the contemplative nuns and monks, you get the feeling they look on them as a luxury the present age can't afford. What they don't see is that prayer is a work, the most necessary of all and a man called to the contemplative life has work to do without which we in the world couldn't do ours properly.

But how exactly does prayer relate to the needs of the world?

I find that the more you practise the different forms of prayer, the more you discover that you're identifying yourself with the whole world. St Paul says, 'Pray for prisoners as if you were a prisoner yourself' (Heb 13:3) – now I find that quite striking and try to apply it to my intercessory prayers. During the course of the day I just float around the 270 Homes, plus other projects and people – and briefly picture each one, like our Home in Katpadi in India for burnt-out leprosy sufferers.

We battled and battled for four years to get it going and I've got the deepest affection for it. I think of the early days with Mrs Chinnadorai. She was a local lady, a widow, a large lady. She had a rickshaw with a man who bicycled her around. She was just like a mother to me. I can't say that I enjoyed all the food she gave me but she went to infinite trouble to get what she thought was most suitable for me, infinite trouble. We had to find a house that we could rent because all I had to spare was thirty pounds. We found houses, but every time the owner discovered what we were going to use them for, he withdrew the deal, or the neighbours forced him to.

Eventually we found a very suitable one, partly occupied by squatters. The owner let us have it and we moved in. I lived there for quite a long time in a tiny little room. One of the leprosy patients, an older man, insisted on sleeping on the floor outside my door, to keep the snakes out, he said. We had such fun together. There was an Anglo-Indian who used to sing beautifully, and when there was the opportunity and we were sitting round the inner courtyard, perhaps in the evening, he and the others used to sing. His favourite song was 'Coming in with a Wing and a Prayer' and I can picture

the way he used to sing it to this day. We bought a
rickshaw for one of them and he used it despite his
disability, to go out on errands for the Home. He even
took paying passengers and gave the money to the
Home. Once we got the Home expanded, we turned
one big room into a dormitory and to my surprise, I
found the beds all built in cement. They were like bus
seats back to back. Kept the bugs out! They can't have
been very comfortable for the patients but they seemed
to like it.

You can imagine, I'm sure, how fond my memories are of that place. But I pause there only a few
seconds, because my job is not to wallow in memories,
my job is to unite myself with them, bring them into the
presence of the good Lord, and pray that if they have
problems they'll be solved, but it's also a two-way
giving, because I find that doing that gives me real
strength; I can't explain it, but I feel that I'm sharing
their struggle, they're helping me on my way and it
gives me an even deeper love for them. Those moments
give me an added impetus in whatever job I'm doing,
whatever new Home I'm opening. At this particular
moment it's Moscow – suddenly last week I was told
they have a property, and have asked me to go and see
it. I've got a fur hat to keep my head warm. Usually I
try to learn a word or two of the language, but not this
time. I'm just trying to adapt myself to the Soviet way
of doing things and generally preparing myself, I hope,
in prayer. Then, besides my Homes, there are countries
in trouble, prisoners, the drug traffic, abortion, the dead.
The longer you go in this form of prayer, the more you
feel a deep desire to identify with everybody, if only
you could.

Oh by the way, we've been talking about praying

for people. Well I'm slightly afraid of that, because that
'for' can sound a bit patronising and I don't mean that
at all. I wouldn't like it to come across in such a way
that I thought I was bestowing a favour on people by
praying for them. I think the point is that prayer brings
you closer to God provided that, when you pray, your
life begins to conform itself to what God wants of you
and it isn't just an abstract activity. I just know from
my limited experience that, the closer you come to
God, the closer you come to your neighbour and understand his needs in a much clearer way.

*But there are very immediate problems, like poverty
and homelessness in London. How can prayer help
here, when it might be better just to go out and do
something for them?*

It's an interesting thing that, when it came to the
Reformation, the first people to see perfectly clearly
what was happening – without going into the rights and
wrongs of it – were the Carthusian monks. Henry VIII
recognised that they were his principal enemy and they
were the first martyrs. Now that confirms my view that,
if your life is devoted totally to prayer you're going to
see the fundamental issues of the world more clearly.
You're like a watchman on a tower. People say, 'Well
how can a man that lives all his life in a monastery
know anything about sex or about human relations, but
the truth is that I find the advice they give me in all
sorts of areas is the best advice I get anywhere. And a
true man or woman of prayer is more dangerous –
much more dangerous to Satan. Satan will be very
active in a monastery. Despite their commitment, they
can have great relationship problems in monasteries –

understandable when you get people locked up together all the time, never getting away.

Now, if you're living in the world, I would argue that you must be an activist, but your action must be underpinned by prayer because it's prayer that gives your words and your actions power and direction. You've got to take action, yes, but it's got to be the right action. For instance I think that the problem of homelessness is a very major one that needs to be addressed properly by society. I feel uneasy about it. The fact, for example, that there are so many homeless in London – and so many of them young – ought really to alert us to finding out the basic cause. Recently I had a discussion about it with a small group and found that there were three contradicting views on what to do. That all showed me how little I myself understood it. Quite often I meet a man outside Westminster Cathedral, who puts his hands out for money. Now, is he going to go straightaway and spend it on drink, or is he genuinely somebody who has nothing to eat? It's clear we must act responsibly towards our neighbour in need and I find myself in a great dilemma. I'm coming to the view that, if we prayed more, we'd be better equipped to judge.

When you see little children at traffic lights in India, knocking on car windows, you can be pretty certain that they are part of an organised structure and I've discovered that some communities of leprosy sufferers there are highly organised; they form themselves into a little society in which each has a specific role: the most helpless-looking one with the greatest deformity does the begging and the one with the least deformity does the buying. There's quite a high membership fee. The other day, I had a letter from a priest in India who had written some while ago with a very appealing story

that his aide needed a motorbike; that seems a very
little thing to give somebody. But I wrote back and
asked him the question, 'How many other people have
you written to?' And he gave me a list of six, so now,
with far more demands than I have any hope of answering, I have to take a decision: how high a priority do I
give him? I've come to realise that some individuals
with access to address lists systematically write around.
Then the word gets round who gives and you find
yourself getting an increasing number of requests. I
ended by referring all letters to our nearest Home to
investigate. I've only got a limited amount of money
and I've got a duty to the people who've given it. If I
give everywhere I'll end up with nothing and that's
when I'll probably meet someone in real need. But
there are cases that haunt me when I've not given and I
can see today clearly in my eye. Once, in Calcutta,
suddenly in front of me was a leprosy sufferer on his
haunches. He fixed me with his eyes and I was so taken
by his shocking deformity and the intensity of his stare,
that I took a photograph of him and I was so concentrating on the photograph, a good one, which in fact we
used for fund-raising for leprosy, that I walked away
and never gave him anything. You see that's the way
we are, we're human beings. But I don't think it matters
all that much if you get it a bit wrong. So long as you
have a genuine intention to do the right thing.

   The problems of the world are very complex; I take
two or three that I think I understand and get involved in
them. I got involved with the Sunday trading debate and
I did with the abortion debate in the sense of writing a
personal letter to the Prime Minister, though I can't do
that too often because if you go for too many causes you
lose credibility, don't you. People say, 'There he goes

again!' So instead of spending my time trying to understand the others, I'd rather spend it praying about them. When I disputed with Bruce Kent over the nuclear issue, he put his argument and I put mine and at the end of it I said, 'When all's said and done, the most important thing is to pray.' Now he hotly refuted that, and two other priests came up to me afterwards and said, 'You were quite wrong there – prayer is not a substitute for social action.' I know they are more men of prayer than I am, but they must have been thinking that I meant just going away and saying prayers about the nuclear debate. That isn't what I meant at all. I meant that by developing your prayer life and making it influence the whole conduct of your life, you're going to see the nuclear debate in the way that God sees it and you're going to know better what to do about it.

I don't believe any more in praying for the solution that I think is the right one. If I'm in a jam, my tendency is to say, 'Please God help me, get me out of this.' That's good up to a point, but what's far more important is to know what God wants for me out of this. If every time we prayed for a solution we were given it, then religion would be a career. No, the most fundamental reason for prayer is to understand God's purpose (Matthew 6:9-10,33). A problem could be a symptom of something much deeper, and, were it removed, I might pay no attention to the basic cause, whereas so long as it's there it may be making me think more deeply about it.

I also contemplate the mystery of Creation – why was it that God who lacks nothing came to create us, who do nothing really but cause trouble? It must mean that he so longs to be giving that he has to pour himself out into something that is nothing, us. That's the extraordinary thing. It's almost as if he can't do without us. He's like a father with a little child. The child asks for something and the father can't help giving it to him as long as it's not something harmful. The closer we can come to God through prayer the more we can respond to the love that he gives us, the more we become channels through which the power, the gentle power of his love can reach those who as yet do not know him. And the closer you come to God, the more you realise your dependence on other people and also the more you realise your own shortcomings and your own dependence on God.

What about the Nagasaki anniversary – when you went off to pray quietly instead of joining the official ceremony? What motivated you there?

The City Council of Nagasaki said they wouldn't allow me to go to the peace ceremony on the grounds that they couldn't guarantee my safety. A queer kind of peace ceremony! But it was my good fortune, because rather than sitting for a long time in a hot tent listening to a lot of speeches in Japanese, most of them, I understand, trying to make a political point, I had an hour completely on my own in the oldest church in Japan, built by the French on top of a little hill. For me it was a day charged with memories and conflicting emotions; the anniversary of the end of World War Two and I was standing in the very place where the end had come. I longed to be alone with my thoughts, for at least a while. The solitude and quiet of that church was an absolute God-send, a tiny haven of silence in a noisy and bustling world in which it's all too easy to forget the power of prayer.

In your travels, you must have had a lot of encounters with the non-Christian faiths. Have they in any way influenced the way you pray?

Their commitment and asceticism impresses me a lot, but between Eastern forms of meditation and Christianity there's a fundamental difference. They are seeking by their own individual efforts to remove themselves from the bonds of matter and enter a pure, spiritual state, but the Christian sees God as the beginning and end of everything, he sees himself as unable to do anything except through God, so he's looking to God to lift him up. Equally, he sees everything God made as good, here too there is a fundamental difference. At the same time it's obvious there's a lot of good in the way Buddhists, Hindus and others live their beliefs – but in all Eastern or transcendental meditation techniques I see the attraction but I also see the danger for the Christian, that he comes to see the particular technique, not the power of God as the key.

There seems to be more emphasis on community prayer in the modern Church, but you seem to prefer to pray as an individual.

I like to pray as an individual, but I would prefer to do my period of silence in the company of others. It's quite clear we're not brought to salvation individually but with the whole community of the human family. But I don't take easily, for instance, to joining hands and being in a group where everybody's spontaneously saying their own extemporary prayers, like some of the Charismatics. It's my nature I suppose, I'm reserved. I admire it and respect it and I know it's right for some people, but it's not my way. I just feel slightly ill at ease with it.

Could you say a bit more about the prayer of silence, or, as you call it, the 'Prayer of the Heart'? Why is it so important to you?

It was only in the last five or six years that I came to the prayer of silence, and that was through going back to the Carthusians at Parkminster. That made a huge difference to me, because I think the Church has concentrated so much on the set prayers, the vocal prayers, the Divine Office and so on, that personal, silent prayer has been pushed a little into the background. But that's changing fast. It took a year, perhaps, before silent prayer became a part of me and I found this greatly deepened my awareness of the presence of God, made more personal my relationship with him and I think has given me more insights into the Faith. It's also helped me understand that any improvement I can make in myself is in fact a tiny improvement in the whole of humanity.

The Prayer of the Heart means that the mind descends to the heart. You bring all the dispositions of your being, your mind, your memory, your will, your feelings and emotions and passions into the centre of your being, so that the total person is there, attentive, alert, humble, silent, watching and listening, not making any move of your own, but just using a little formula which people sometimes call a mantra – though I personally think the mantra idea is sometimes overdone. Its purpose is to help you remain recollected, silently in the presence of God. It's a prayer where I enter the inner room of my being. God dwells there anyway, but he's free to move about in it only in so far as I allow him and in so far as my house is in order. There are areas of our being that we reserve to ourselves and don't want others, even God, to know about. He's always working within us for our own good and in his own mysterious way, but in the prayer of silence, he has the freedom to work in a way he can't when our minds and our bodies are active. He has a twofold job to do: he's got to burn away all the impurities, open the dark corners and let the light in. He's also recreating us into the new creation that he intends us to become. If I remain like this, silent, watchful, humble, he'll work unseen, leaving no footprints, perhaps allowing me to feel that I'm just sitting like a dope, wasting my time. I can go through a forty-five minute period with my mind all over the place, but when the alarm on my wrist-watch which I set for forty-five minutes goes off, I nearly always find myself wishing it could be longer. The importance, I think, is that I've tried, however poorly, to put myself at God's disposal. Perhaps the fact of having done it very badly helps us understand a little better how mortal we are, how little we can do without him.

There are times when it's quite different; I think of God, totally outside and other than his creation, yet living within me as if I was the only person that mattered, and I think 'How can that be?' I know it's impossible but I still get a sort of longing to catch a little glimpse of him. I also begin to realise that almost his most fundamental attribute is beauty and I think, if there's so much beauty, even in a world gone wrong, then what must the Creator be? There's beauty in people, in human relationships, and in the things that people do. I was at a reception at which a Professor of

Mathematics had been going round from group to group with a look of wonder on his face at a mathematical discovery he had just made, and I can't forget Gigi my daughter bubbling over at the bemused look on the faces of those on whom he was letting loose his discovery! When I met a leading mathematician at a Merton College dinner, I asked him what it was that had attracted him in Maths. Without any hesitation, he said, 'Beauty'.

Side by side with beauty go awe and wonder, and if there's one reaction we ought to have when contemplating God, it's wonder. We should be lost in wonder. There was a Franciscan out in Dehra Dun who used to make his hour's meditation every morning on the verandah to his flowers. In those days I used to think it was rather eccentric and peculiar, but I don't think so any more. They're beautiful and they're God's creation and one man has one inspiration and another has another.

I love animals – and birds especially. When I was a child we always had a dog and in the Air Force I had a poodle and a cat. Animals give you a sense of joy as God's beautiful little creatures. Everything in the entire Creation in its own way reflects God. The reason that I've pieced together that evolution chart in my room is that the whole of creation has a deep meaning for me. I want to understand a little better how we are part of the whole cosmos. We've come out of what four and a half billion years ago was a seething mass of molten matter and it's our task to build it up into the masterpiece of harmony, beauty and joy that God has in mind.

I'm not trying to say that the Prayer of the Heart is the most important kind of prayer, but it is an essential prayer. All prayers deepen our relationship with God, but its particular purpose is to make that relationship perfect, to make me into a person who will listen to that little inner voice, who will notice the things around me, little things that call for my attention when the bigger, more attractive thing in the shop window is distracting me. A man of prayer is the man whose work becomes a prayer.

And is that a description of yourself?

No! I'm talking about the perfect man of prayer. That's far from talking about myself. Please understand that. You can know what you should be, but you can be miles and miles away from it and I know with no artificiality that that is where I am.

You've now combined your feelings about the Prayer of Silence with your contacts with the disabled in what you call your 'Family of Prayer' – from where did the inspiration for that come?

The Family of Prayer is based on watching, which comes very frequently into Scripture. I can't get over the fact that Jesus turned to Peter, James and John at Gethsemane and said, 'Stay here and watch with me' (Mark 14:32-41; Matthew 26:36-41), and they didn't. He didn't ask them to pray, but to watch. It says the Garden of Olives, but the point, I think, is that there was an olive press there, which actually crushed the olives to drain their oil. And he was psychologically crushed to the point where his sweat turned to blood. Well that cry, 'Couldn't you watch with me just one hour,' (Matthew 26:40) goes down the ages as a personal plea, and I wanted somehow to answer it.

One thing that stands out for me is the general assertion in the Church that Jesus, in his life and particularly in his passion and death, shared in every form of suffering that human beings have suffered. At the back of our Home for mentally handicapped children at Pritam Road, Dehra Dun, was a walled-in area, not exactly a garden, but with a little bit of grass, and it was while living there that I began to think that – and it's only a personal supposition – at Gethsemane, in some way that we don't understand, Jesus was sharing the sufferings of the mentally handicapped. I talked about it, anyway part of it, to Gracie Abel, the Indian lady who had run the Home from the very beginning and is still working in it today at the age of 83 and found her so receptive that we agreed to plant an olive tree - we managed to find one in Dehra Dun – in the walled-in space and call it the olive garden. Gracie, who's a Christian, if not a regular church-goer, always refers to it. And this year was the first year it had actual olives, a really beautiful crop. So that was my first step.

My first thought had been a specially designed kind of monastery for disabled people. But the more I thought about it the more I saw the practical difficulties. It was only three years ago that, having come to adopt the Prayer of the Heart, I began to see the idea in a different light – not in terms of a place, but as a very simple rule based on our Lord's cry for help at Gethsemane, applied to people wherever they might be living.

Now watching, I think, is the equivalent to being on sentry guard. Remember in the temptation in the desert, the devil left Jesus, 'until the appointed time' (Luke 4:13). And when the appointed time came there was a feeling of danger in the air, that the forces of

darkness were mustering and were converging on Jesus. And he said to his disciples, 'Watch'. We should be
on the look-out for an evil prompting, we should be on
the look-out for somebody who needs our help, and
above all we should be watchful for what we think God
is inviting us to do. You can see a wild animal asleep;
absolutely, totally asleep, but if there's a sudden emer-
gency, it can be fully alert, bounding away with energy
and ready for anything in a split second. You've got to
be ready at any moment for something unexpected and
be able to respond.

So for the Family of Prayer there are only two
requirements: one that you agree to set aside a minimum of an hour in the week for silent prayer in response to Our Lord's plea at Gethsemane. Second,
since the spirit of Gethsemane is one of loving submis-
sion to the will of God (John 17) no matter how difficult the circumstances, you must make a resolve to
accept whatever God sends, not only with love but with
reverence. Cardinal Hume and Cardinal Cassidy at the
Vatican, once Chairman of our Home in Dhaka, have
approved it and it's very slowly growing, but without
our trying to push it. Our members are probably less
than a hundred but they are in different countries. The
great help is that one can't easily do it all on one's own.
Knowing others are doing it too makes a great difference.

*Have you never argued with God? If something's gone
wrong, have you ever said, 'I'm a thinking person –
why are you doing this to me?'*

Yes, I've complained about things that have happened, but I'm not quite so sure that I've put them in

my prayers, which I should have done. You may think I have accepted everything, but I certainly have not. I find that I can accept the big things, that's quite easy – suddenly being told that you've got TB and that you're likely to be in bed for the next two years. It's the small things that trip me up. But God always wins in the end.

And what part does penance play in your life?

I'm a little dubious about penances – the danger is that a penance becomes a penance for the sake of it and you get rather pleased about it. I think that, far more important than penance, is self-denial. Accepting with good grace duties I don't want to undertake, people who come and ask me something that's most inconvenient. That's better than restricting myself to one cup of coffee a day, or before I know where I am, I'm going through mental agony every time I want a cup of coffee. That's a silly position to get into. We do have to restrain the impulses of the body; there has to be some going without. I'm just not quite sure I've got it right in my own case.

In a way, the more you pray, the more you realise how little you pray, and how much prayer should be a part of you just as breathing is, not forced. Prayer is a work. You have to work at it. It isn't going to come easily. I think, also, you have to mean it totally. You can say, 'Well I'm going to give prayer a very important part in my life and make sure that other things don't interfere' but that's definitely not enough. Perhaps that's badly put, but prayer really should be at the very top of our priorities, for its goal is nothing less than God himself.

8
Travel

India – Bangladesh – Japan – Hong Kong
– China – Hong Kong – Home

Cheshire's Far East itinerary over four weeks in 1989

I'd be interested to know how you spend a couple of your travelling days. Let's take your recent trip to India.

On the first part of the trip, Sue was with me. We arrived in Delhi roughly at midnight ready for a full two-day programme. There was our Home to visit, with ninety disabled people, a lot of whom are very severely mentally handicapped children, so the first thing was to go round and see each of them. They have a very active workshop to which disabled people come from the surrounding countryside. We spent two or three hours meeting the helpers and the staff. Then there was the new TB project to launch – we in the West tend to think that TB is under control; there's a lot of focus on leprosy, malaria and cancer but TB is almost a forgotten disease. Yet there are ten million sufferers in India alone and it's active and endemic in the slums of Delhi and most of the other big cities. It's found in the rural areas, and particularly in the foothills of the Himalayas around Raphael and presumably all along the whole range. So, over many years, we've been operating a mobile unit, trying to discover a way of reaching and treating the TB sufferer economically.

We had a lunch in aid of the Memorial Fund at the Delhi Golf Club. The second morning we had twenty minutes with the Prime Minister, Rajiv Gandhi. The election was coming up in about three weeks' time and it was extraordinary how relaxed he was. As a boy, he'd been at the Doon School – that's the big public school of India at Dehra Dun, which sent working parties to Raphael, so he'd come over and helped. He's been particularly warm and friendly towards the Homes. But this time we were talking about the Memorial Fund and he'd personally given five thousand pounds to it, as well as writing a very nice message, which was going to be read out at the launch later that evening. Obviously we don't go and see the Prime Minister every visit – that would be completely out of proportion – but, starting with Jawaharlal Nehru, then Indira Gandhi and Rajiv Gandhi, they've all been extremely kind in giving us time and coming out to see the different Homes. I've never forgotten meeting with Nehru. Both my wife and I were on our best behaviour, saying how honoured and pleased we were and Nehru turned round and said, 'Don't be so protocol! Let's sit down and have a nice cup of tea together.' And then, a little later, I approached him about the concept of the hospital we intended to build at Raphael and he said something quite remarkable: 'If you want my blessing, build it small and build it simple. People in this country have a habit of building a great big, very expensive hospital and when they've got it built, they haven't got the money to run it properly.' And when you think that an Indian Minister of Health once told me, 'If I say, "Vote for me and I'll build you a five hundred-bed hospital," I'll get votes, but if I say, "I'll give all villages a protected water supply and proper drainage," I'll get no votes, so what do I do?' It was an extraordinarily honest and perceptive thing for Nehru, in those early days in 1959, to say what he did. It shows the foresight he had.

When it came to the launch of the Memorial Fund, we were astonished at the size – I thought the launch at the new Parliament building in Australia had been a big occasion, but this was far bigger. It was in the largest hall in Delhi. The banner right across the street must have been twenty foot long and ten foot high and there were 800 people there; the chiefs of all three Services, three leading politicians and a complete cross-section of the people of Delhi. Of course this was the crucial moment because it was televised. I had to make the inaugural speech and I had to get it right. In fact, I got it wrong, I did everything except explain what the Memorial Fund was! But it turned out to be a blessing in giving the speaker who came after me, the administrator, a retired very senior army general, his opportunity to explain and that worked out all right. There was a radio interview with Mark Tully of the BBC, two interviews with the press, another interview with television, so we were very fortunate in the way that launch started and, in fact, within the first week of the launch, they'd collected £25,000. They've set themselves a goal of two million pounds, and they seem confident that they're going to get that. So that was quite a big day in terms of success, but fairly average in terms of things to be fitted in.

After it, we trundled up on the overnight train to Dehra Dun on the way to Raphael. Raphael is something completely special because it's a 'village' of Homes: what we used to call the leprosy colony, now called Shiv Sadan after the first Chairman; the unit for the mentally retarded, Ava Vihar after dear Mrs Ava Dhar, our first administrator; the 'Little White House', which is the orphanage for children that are either orphans or come from leprosy parents, children who, if they grew up with their parents, couldn't marry outside the leprosy world, and other children who for one reason or another can't live satisfactorily at home. And we have the hospital unit, with the chronic ward and the TB ward. And there's also the mobile TB unit. When we come to Raphael, everything is organized from start to finish in a fantastic way. You start with the hundred

leprosy patients lining each side of the 150-yard approach road. And as you go along, you greet each one
and every second or third one puts a garland round your
neck till it's so heavy that you have to bend down and
take a few off. Many, to your embarrassment, kneel
down and clasp your feet. It's all smiles and there are
three men with drums who start a rhythm up and sing
and yodel and finally dance and you begin to dance
after a fashion too. Well I can't sing but I can at least
move my feet about! When you've made your way
slowly along them and waved good-bye, you meet the
little children and then you meet the mentally retarded,
then you meet the TB patients and so on, I don't quite
know how to put it; it may sound rather ostentatious but
it isn't, it comes from the heart both ways, like meeting
the family after a long time away. Raphael is a family to
us, we've known it and loved it so long.

The welcomes over, a short closed session with
Rummy Bakhshi and Shoba his wife to be briefed on
the programme and a moment to settle into our room.
Rummy is a retired General who won the MC* in
Burma and twelve years ago took over as Raphael's
Administrator on a temporary basis. He's been there
ever since, firmly but gently in control, loved and looked
up to by everybody. Then lunch – everybody sits down
on the grass in the garden in front of the Little White
House. And then Rummy Bakhshi puts a little table up
where he and his wife sit with us. There are so many
people and things to see, we can't both do everything.
This time, my wife spent the day driving out with the
mobile TB unit, while I went around Raphael itself,
unit by unit, seeing everybody and catching up with

* Military Cross

their news. In addition to that, we always have a formal meeting with the leprosy patients which follows a well laid down pattern. Rummy takes charge with Sue and me at either side of him behind a trestle table. First we ask them if they've got anything they want to talk about and they'll come out with one or two or three requests and complaints which are knocked back and forth between us until we all come to a happy compromise. On this occasion they said to me, 'It's all very well; you sit here, Captain Sahib and Mem Sahib and solve the problem, but then you go and we have to carry on our battles with the General.' So I said, 'Well, when you have your battles with the General, who wins, you or the General?' They all thought this was hugely funny. You've got this lovely mixture; they come out with their complaints or requests – they want another set of clothing or something, they shout and wave their fists, sometimes go for each other, yet it's all so friendly and informal and always ends with three cheers: 'Memsahib Hip Hip.... Group Captain Sahib Hip Hip...' On the second day we had the staff tea, under the trees outside the hospital block, with all the Class Two staff, as they're called, the servants. They pointed out that their wages were very low, which they are, compared with what they get in hospitals. And, as usual, we had to say that, unfortunately, we couldn't succeed in raising more. We were doing all we could; so were Australia and New Zealand, from where most of Raphael's money came. We'd continue trying and, please God, one day would succeed.

Then towards the end, there's always a concert when every little department of Raphael puts on its own show and this time the standard was more remarkable than ever. It was a particularly attractive light –

towards four in the afternoon and the sun getting lower.
The flowers were all blooming and all the important
people of Dehra Dun as well as all the community were
there. That's the lovely thing about Raphael; there must
be four hundred living there and yet they can reduce
these big events to a family occasion.

After calling on a special friend, Nan Pandit,*
whom we had known when she was High Commissioner in London, we got on the night train again and
went back to Delhi. We had a meeting with Dr Pamra,
the internationally known TB specialist, 82 but still
going all round the world attending conventions and,
mercifully for us, helping our TB operations. Then we
went to see the British High Commissioner. They have
always been so friendly to us, the present one, Sir
David Goodall especially so. My wife had to leave
early to be driven to the airport to go to Nepal to visit
our centre there, her first visit, while I caught a later
plane to get to Bangladesh.

*That sort of hectic life all sounds very enjoyable – but
what about the difficulties?*

Of course those journeys have their practical problems. Every one is different, depending on which part
of the world you're going to, but usually it's a multiple
journey, so you've got some areas where you're living
out in the wilds, while at one stage or another of the
journey, you may be staying at Government House or
the Embassy. Therefore one of my problems is knowing what sort of clothes to take, in a minimum space, so

* Mrs Vijaya Lakshmi Pandit, Nehru's sister, who died on 1 December
1990

I can be properly dressed for each function. It rarely happens now, but one thing I don't like is being unpacked. In her early days in Germany, my wife once stayed with the British Army Corps Commander in Germany. She'd had a quick lunch, while driving, of two bananas and, not finding a waste paper basket, she had shoved the skins into her suitcase. When she got to her room she found the maid had unpacked her clothes and neatly laid out the banana skins on the dressing table!

The other problem when you go to a new country altogether is to decide whether to make contact with the British Embassy or High Commission. My general policy is not to, because I don't want to be a nuisance to the unfortunate Ambassador who's got plenty to do without my problems landing on his desk. On the other hand, sometimes you need advice or feel it's right and proper to put them in the picture. And it's interesting, looking back over these thirty years, how different the response can be. Almost always we get a warm welcome and positive support from the Embassy or High Commission, sometimes overwhelmingly so, but there have been occasions in the beginning, when we were unknown, and still occasionally today, when things have been rather different.

I remember when my wife, who drives everywhere by car, usually on her own, had been specially asked to call in at a Central European Embassy to report about something. She'd driven overnight from Warsaw non-stop, and arrived at the Embassy a little early for working hours, so she'd had to wait. In came an official and asked what she wanted. No one seemed to know about the message. She wasn't offered a cup of coffee or even a glass of water – the way she described

it was, 'I felt as if I was something the cat had brought
in!' I suppose it never occurred to that official that
she'd driven through the night, though he or the Reception ought to have noticed she looked a bit the worse
for wear! That's an isolated case, but there are times
when you definitely feel that you'd have done better
not to have come in.

On the other hand, some of the help that we've
had from ambassadors has been quite extraordinary. At
least three of our Homes have been started purely on
the initiative of the local Ambassador or High Commissioner, and at this very moment the embassy in Liberia
has gone to considerable inconvenience and risk to
rescue the nine surviving severely handicapped children in our Home over-run by the fighting. Ambassadors and High Commissioners go on helping us in their
retirement, too, to our great advantage.

*When you set up in a new country, your philosophy has
been to try to become part of its culture, and to work in
partnership. But it must be difficult, sometimes, to cir-
cumvent cultural differences – and avoid politics. In
Japan, for example, in view of your past history, did
you find you faced any problems or opposition?*

Far from it. In fact there has actually been the
most extraordinary help. Our work in Japan was set up
by Katarina Thome, a Norwegian girl who went to
Japan with virtually no introductions at the age of only
twenty-one – having learnt Japanese in only five months.
Within a year she had set up our first Home near Kobe.
My first visit there coincided with the BBC taking me
to Nagasaki for the fortieth anniversary programme
and they covered my visit to the Home on camera. That

meant that everybody there knew where I was going but to my recollection it didn't enter into the conversation. Certainly it made no difference whatsoever to our relationship or their response. My role at Nagasaki had nothing to do with it at all in their eyes. Absolutely none. The only thing that they were interested in was that this was a new concept for the residential care of disabled people.

They'd had nothing like it before. They had very fine facilities for disabled people but not a family-type home. Last year (1989) I had to go and address a meeting of people running social welfare. And they asked me some quite poignant questions about freedom. Most of their organisations are government-run and because of this, the homes have to do everything according to set rules and that, in some cases, militates against the freedom of the residents. I had to answer fairly diplomatically because it was a government-organised meeting, but I nevertheless spoke about risk-taking. You see, a disabled person tends to be sheltered and protected. In Japan, they are not allowed to let somebody go out on their own. It gave me the opportunity to put our conclusion, which is that you must come down in favour of letting the disabled person take a risk, even though you think it's a dangerous one, so long as it's not totally reckless or wilful.

It was a learning experience for me. I began to learn that they do things quite differently from us and that the way I was putting things across was the wrong way in Japan. What you've got to do is first state the general objective: 'I am involved in an organisation caring for disabled people. I am its founder. Our work consists in residential Homes. We have them in various countries. Amongst the countries that we have is Japan.

The way in which the Home operates is that and that.'
And with the Memorial Fund, the way I put it across in
Britain was, 'I'm looking for five pounds for each of
the lives lost in the two World Wars.' Now, if you do
that in Japan, you're lost from the word go. For one
thing, remembrance doesn't mean anything like as much
to them as it does to us. Secondly, you should give the
general picture and then work your way down. And the
third thing is that the head of an organisation does not
take decisions; all decisions are collective. I'm probably over-generalising, but it actually was very good
for me because it taught me to be precise and logical.

Then I discovered that, in Japan, you get very
good marks for persistence. At the Social Services, they
kept referring to Katarina and saying that the corridors
resounded with the sound of her voice and who was
this young girl, (tall and blonde and very striking looking), who never gave them any peace? So the fact that
she kept going back opened the door for her. It's the
same with me and the Memorial Fund. At first I had
'no' at every entry point. Always no, no, no. But I keep
going in, at different levels, different directions, different people. I know that, in the end, Japan will be a
major donor and I know that I've got to keep going.

The design of our new Home in Japan – it's unbe-
lievable. And the speed with which they put it up!
During my first visit in 1984, they showed me the site
they wanted to acquire in August. I got a letter saying,
'The Home, for forty-four residents, is going to be
completed and ready for opening in June. Will you
please come to the opening!' In England it would be at
least 18 months, probably two years.

On my second visit, I had some time to sit with the
residents. Just sitting with them. I was close to them. I

could put out my hand and they could hold my hand. I'll never forget those twenty minutes or so, just realising that, unable to communicate a single word (I may know six words of Japanese but it doesn't get you very far), you can establish a real relationship and I can still feel it now. There we were in a totally different culture and one that tends to be a closed society, the only island in the world that's never been invaded. And the Christmas cards I've had from them! That really reflects it. Those international contacts with the disabled have taught me something important about our common humanity.

If you take the China Home, that was completely new territory. I hadn't been there before. I've spent a lot of time in India – I don't say I know how the Indians think, but I know a good deal about them and I'm at home with them. But here I was in China, the big stranger from abroad. If you are old, that gives you a stronger position; they respect age. There was a lot of protocol, a lot of VIP treatment. You've got to observe the protocol and respond in a dignified way. But at the same time, you have to break through and get onto a more human understanding. And it was one of those occasions which worked. To begin with, there was Deng Pufang, the son of Deng Xiaoping, the Chinese leader – a controversial figure now. But Deng Pufang, his son, was in a wheelchair. He had opposed the Cultural Revolution as an undergraduate, while his father had the sense to lie low, and he was tortured and thrown out of a window. I had met him three times before and we had been very polite to each other, but had only had a short conversation. This time, I came into the reception room, with the television cameras and glaring lights and there was Deng Pufang in his chair looking at me, and he had such a lovely welcoming look and warmth and happiness in his eyes because the project had come about – I'll never forget that look – that I felt strongly drawn to him, and before I knew what was happening, we were embracing each other. I spent the morning at the Home. I couldn't speak to the residents, but again we could just sit together in a little circle and hold hands, or put arms round each other.

Something concerns me though – one of the aims behind establishing your homes has been to help build a better world, a form of peace building. But you are dealing at the moment with the regime which, only recently committed the terrible atrocities against the demonstrators in Tiananmen Square. Has that been a factor in your thinking? The story of Deng Pufang's welcome was charming, but there's a slightly uneasy thought that it's been something of a propaganda coup for the Chinese to have you going over there. Look at the publicity they gave you.

I'm really doing my work because I feel it's the job that I was given to do. I believe that, in a tiny way, it's helping build up a better world, but only because it's God's total plan for all of us. But going back to your question, there could, I suppose, have been a propaganda element but ... no, I don't believe they even tried; all the talk was around disabled people. Also, Kunming is three thousand kilometers from Beijing.

In a similar way, when we were first invited to go to South Africa, where we've been working for roughly twenty years and have got nine Homes in existence and seven being built, it was contrary to all our basic policies. For example, our Homes have to be racially segregated, we couldn't have them otherwise. So I thought, 'Should I go or should I not?' But when you sit down and think about it for a moment, the answer is obviously yes, because we are solely concerned with helping disabled people towards greater freedom and independence. The fact that there's an unjust or repressive regime at the top – anyway perceived as unjust and repressive – cannot be a reason for not helping the disabled person living under that regime. In fact, in a certain way, there's all the more reason to help them, because, if the regime is oppressive, then their condition is likely to be even worse than in a freer society. I am merely concerned with getting local people to take an interest in providing better care services for their own disabled. I'm careful to do nothing that identifies me with supporting the regime, but neither do I want to attack it, because, if my job is to help the disabled people, I don't want to be provocative. Still, I'm not going to compromise. In South Africa I have a formula which I discussed with Archbishop Hurley of Durban before I went. I don't like giving public talks but if I'm forced to say something, I don't disguise my view about the regime, but I present it in a way that is positive and constructive. You see, with South Africa, it's all very well saying that they are unjust. They are, but if that's all you are going to say, then you won't get very far, because there is also a lot of good in them. And if you don't acknowledge the good, then you merely drive the person into a corner. Whatever happens, never say anything that is exaggerated or unfair, because if you do, as I know from my own experience, they seize on that. I think it's a great gift to be able to tell a man straight and squarely where he's wrong but in such a way that you also give him credit and acknowledge the difficulties he's facing and you give him nothing that he can latch onto as being unjust. And above all, you must offer hope. I think we tend to fall down in that respect with South Africa. We do nothing but criticise.

The best way seems to be to refer to the fact that there's a major problem in South Africa. There's no need to say what the problem is, because everybody knows that. And then to say that, in a way, South Africa has the problems that every country has, though in a very concentrated form. And I also assert that, when the day comes that the problems are resolved, when every individual in South Africa is given equal rights, without destroying the fabric of South African society, then South Africa will have an immense role to play in the family of nations. In fact, I even think that, if she can once get those problems solved, South Africa is the natural leader of Africa. The other formula that I used on one occasion, a musical evening, was to draw the analogy with an orchestra. Other people of course have used this, but I said that what makes a concert is the diversity of the different instruments and notes, all combined into one melody and that is really a little analogy of how the human family should be. Without the widely differing notes, small as well as big, you don't get the full, rich effect of the melody.

I have known one anti-apartheid campaigner in London who was very vocal and committed but when blacks started to move into his street, he joined the protest against them. You see, the black people coming into his street suddenly hit him personally. He thought it devalued his property. You can be very pious and clean and reforming on the other side of the ocean and you don't see that the white in South Africa has a legitimate fear. He thinks, perhaps wrongly, but he thinks, 'If we give all the blacks, something like 23 million of them against three million of us, control of this country, we'll be in the sea, and all we and our forebears have struggled for and achieved will go.' I know very few men who would be willing to lower their standard of living to help the poor. I don't think that the anti-South African campaigners try to understand that side of it. I think I ought to make the point that I don't believe that we can correct injustice anywhere in the world without being willing to give up something ourselves, anyway in the short term. That may very well mean a drop in your standard of living. There comes the problem.

But has starting the Homes in South Africa done more than just help the disabled people who live in them?

I can honestly say that it has, marginally I know, but nevertheless it has. All the regional committees for the Homes are now racially mixed. I know you can say that's only on the periphery; it is. But nevertheless, it's one tiny bridge and I'd far rather spend my years building little bridges through my Homes, than to be isolating myself from the country because it's an oppressive regime and trying to confront the regime by public demonstration. I'm not saying that the public demonstrations and the sanctions may not be needed, but it's not my job.

Now last year, 1989, we had our International Week in London. We had delegates that included disabled people and staff and committee members from over 35 countries and they all had to share rooms at the Tara Hotel, because we couldn't afford to have single rooms. The two disabled people who came from South

Africa were Corrie, who's white, and Patrick, who's black, and they had to share the same room. Now that wouldn't really be thinkable in South Africa. They didn't really know each other very much before, but everybody noticed the friendship between them. And by the time we had the final reception given by Nicholas Scott, the Minister for the Disabled, at Lancaster House, Corrie, who came from Johannesburg and Patrick, who came from Daveyton, a black suburb of Johannesburg had decided that, as soon as they could get organised, they'd set up a little house for disabled living in Daveytown and they'd both live there and invite two others. So I told Nicholas Scott this and he could hardly believe it. I think the story tells itself, doesn't it? I think I should also add that, on every single visit I've made to South Africa, I've seen a change – the communities coming closer together.

On my last visit in August 1990, there was an even more dramatic development. The residents in our white Home in Port Elizabeth said, 'All the time we've been here, we have been looked after by black staff. So why don't we open our doors and invite black residents to come and share our home with us?' That wouldn't really be a solution to the needs of black disabled people, for what we have got to do is provide new accommodation, in other words an entirely new Home. All the same, it does illustrate a completely different attitude of mind from the day, twenty-five years ago, that the first South African Home opened in Durban.

And now you've started up in the Soviet Union. What were your impressions about the situation of the disabled there?

Yes, whenever I spoke about China, and said my long-time dream to start a home there now looked like being fulfilled, nearly everybody immediately said, 'Well what about the Soviet Union?' and I said, 'No that's impossible.' Mother Teresa said,'Well you've beaten me into China!' But of course, to use her own phrase, she's beaten me into the Soviet Union. It never entered my mind that there was the remotest chance. And then suddenly, from nowhere, came the invitation. I followed it with one or two telexes and letters but there was no answer. I thought it was going to be a bit like China, we would have to wait a year before anything happened. But now, suddenly, it's happened – we have a building. The reason why there was no answer was that my contact, Vladimir Alkhimov,* had not been very well. But all the time they'd been searching for a property.

My last trip had two purposes. The first was the Memorial Fund and the second the Home. When we were discussing fund-raising ideas for the Memorial Fund, Alkhimov suddenly offered to give us metal from their scrapped nuclear missiles to make into medallions and sell. I told him that medallions didn't sell in the West but that we would make pens. He then said, 'Please get your American friends to do the same.' Incidentally, that didn't prove quite so easy. My first two appointments in Moscow were with First Deputy Minister Vorontsov and Andrei Kosirev, also in the Foreign Office, where we discussed some of the practicalities and in particular the official press conference at which the announcement about the pens was to be made. I took the occasion to tell him about a scheme I'm very anx-

* Former head of the state bank and former Deputy at the Ministry of Trade and a hero of the Soviet Union

ious to promote through the Memorial Fund – that I felt it was time for the world community to start thinking about establishing a United Nations Disaster Relief Corps along roughly similar lines to the Peacekeeping Corps. The thinking behind that is that, in many areas of disaster relief, the military are far better equipped to respond than anyone else. It would also be good for their morale and their public image, so that they are not always perceived by some people as just preparing for war. Well, Kosirev was really excited about this. He said, 'This is precisely in line with Soviet thinking. We believe that, in future, as far as possible, the use of the military should be placed under United Nations auspices – I don't mean literal command. We never actually thought of that idea, we'll support it to the full.'

Well, Kosirev arranged for me the following day to make the press announcement about the pens in the official press room of the Ministry of Foreign Affairs. And I must say, when I walked into the room and looked at that platform which I had seen so often on TV and realised I would be speaking from it, I could hardly believe it. Tass released the news all round the world and it led to a number of letters from countries as far apart as Czechoslovakia, Ethiopia and Argentina.

I met the Deputy Mayor of Baumanski District, in which the Home was to be, met their officials, agreed all the elements of the deal. They would dig the foundations, provide the approach road, lay on the services – gas, electricity, water, sewage – and they would give us the site. It was January, cold and snowing and it was rather isolated. But I was just so happy at getting a site that perhaps my judgement was a bit warped. I then went to a rehabilitation unit and met some of the disabled who were going to go into the Home. That's an experience I won't forget. When I asked the doctor in charge – and it was obviously a very efficient and professional unit – 'Where do the patients go when they've finished here?' He said, 'Nowhere. There's nowhere they can go. They have to go home.' Well, home in Moscow probably means a tiny flat with hardly any room for a wheelchair in a block that, as likely as not, hasn't got a lift. If it has got a lift, the doors open inwards and you wouldn't get a wheelchair in. And if you can get a wheelchair in, you can't shut the door. You never see a disabled person in a wheelchair in the streets of Moscow. I was later told by Russians that somebody in a wheelchair in the street would be treated with hostility. They might even say, 'What have you done to get that disability?' So that was the first thing, the very great need.

There was an extraordinary longing look in the eyes of those disabled people. One of them was an ice hockey player – he was in the junior national team and had broken his neck in an accident playing for his country. He was obviously a strong fellow because he had put on a great deal of weight. His first question to me was, 'Are you allowed to get married in the Homes?' I said, 'Yes, a lot of our residents get married.'

'I am the first man to enter then,' he said – and he put his hand up.

Then two of them said to me about the Home, 'We don't believe it. We've heard this kind of thing too often.' I said, 'Please don't lose faith.' They said, 'Well, if you do build a Home for us, run it, because if you leave it to the bureaucrats, they will destroy it in six months. It will just come to nothing.' So you can see the kind of cynicism, scepticism, that the system must have engendered in that young generation. It gave me an immense longing and an urge to see the Home built.

That deal with the Baumanski District fell through. They had elections a fortnight later. The Deputy Mayor and the Head of the Health Department weren't returned to office, which evidently means in the Soviet Union that everything they had done was cancelled. We were then given another site which was unsuitable because it was too remote. Now, third time lucky, our International Director, Ronald Travers, has secured a firm deal in a really ideal site. So let's hope for the best.

9

Work

For the first ten years of his Foundation, Cheshire took no money from it at all. When he could no longer afford to travel on his pension, the Foundation paid his travelling expenses. Since it's a registered charity, he draws no salary from it. His mother gave him a car in 1959, which he kept for ten years. After that, the Foundation provided him with a car and recently with a driver since he admits he's now no longer safe behind the wheel. He lives, and brought up his children on, his disability pension and his wife's small income, now augmented by an old age pension. He sometimes gives his fees for articles or radio broadcasts to the Homes.

Delegating your work must have meant sacrifices for you – and you also now seem to be living your life very much at a global level. Do you miss the days when it was just you and Arthur and a few disabled people with a very personal relationship, when you could see what you were doing and were close to it?

Of course you say, 'I founded this, this is my baby. He's a very good man, he's doing his best, but he doesn't understand my baby like I do.' Before I got TB, a major crack had developed in the foundations of Le Court. I'd applied to the Carnegie Fund for a van and they came down to have a look. I knew that, whatever happened, I mustn't let them see the crack or they wouldn't give me the van. But I couldn't prevent them seeing it, so I had to admit that the builder had said it had to be pulled down, but added quickly, 'But I don't believe him.' Well it ended up with the Carnegie Fund offering me the money to build a new Home. By this time I was in the sanatorium and once it had all been agreed, they wrote a letter saying, 'We're going to give you the money but on condition that you sign a statement saying you renounce all power over Le Court.' I decided to write to the Committee and say, 'Look, our freedom is more important than £56,000, but somehow I couldn't compose the letter. Post time was coming up; I was getting more and more worked up and I got to the point when I said, 'OK, give in, let it go'; I renounced everything. I felt very sore.' I started it. I got it going. I'm doing no harm with it. I've developed two more Homes. Why should they do this?' But I had no option, and that, really was my saving. I'd relinquished control to the Committee, but in fact I'd lost nothing, because they were still going to listen to me and it released me to roam the world, when I got the opportunity, to start new Homes.

My job has varied over the years. My first job was to get the Homes started and to impart to them enough inner momentum so that they would carry on. Yes I've got to think about future projects. China and the Soviet Union came to me personally, so obviously I'm involved in that, but I couldn't do it single-handed. There's a mass of paperwork and details that I couldn't master any longer, I'm not involved in the nuts and bolts of starting a Home or running the Foundation, but I keep my eye on the fundamentals. And I still hold my principal function is to keep the closest personal contact I can by visiting, sitting quietly for a while with each resident – I try to make that a rule – by keeping up my correspondence, by Christmas cards, by seeing people when they come to England and so on. Yes, I miss the old days in a certain nostalgic sense – you look back to your childhood and they were lovely days – but not in the sense that I wish I could go back to them. I'm looking forward now, at today and tomorrow. The Memorial Fund is a little different. It's still at the beginning. I have to be much more personally involved.

I don't really feel I'm dealing with major issues at top level. I am more concerned with dealing with little individual parts as they affect me. I know sometimes I have to go to a big function, or give a radio interview or sometimes go and see a Prime Minister, but that's not really the essence of my work. If there is a mountain of a problem that faces me, I'd rather get stuck into the bottom with a trowel and begin to shift a bit of earth, than sit back and think, 'How do we move this mountain?'

*It actually must be rather difficult having the reputa-
tion of a person who does a lot of good. Now, be honest,
tell me your faults!*

I do think that, when you're doing the kind of
work I'm doing now, you have to do everything in your
power to make it clear that you haven't got an ulterior
motive. For some people it's social climbing. You're
brought into contact with people you might never otherwise meet. For others it's some kind of public recognition. Or it gives them a position of power – to be on a
committee that's controlling something, otherwise
they'd be leading perfectly ordinary, individual lives.
So you must be very careful. Obviously your motives
are mixed. None of us can honestly say our motives are
totally pure, I know that mine aren't. But I think that
you have to cut out of yourself everything that you
possibly can that might be self-seeking.

I'll tell you what the danger is in the kind of work
that I'm doing – that you begin to think in terms of
'How many Homes have I got? Instead of thinking,
'They're people in need, we must go and help them.'
That is uppermost in my thoughts, but I sometimes
catch myself saying, 'Ah yes, another Home!'

I think that anybody who is, so to speak, a founder,
has difficult traits because your job is to overcome
difficulties, and you tend to see people standing in the
way of what you've got to achieve. With each new
Home, I might have been intolerant if people wanted to
thwart me, or do things differently. It was my whole
life; I was totally devoted to getting that Home started,
to looking after the people that needed to come into it
and I thought I knew what was best for them, while the
committee members were completely new to it. I would

think I was in some ways a difficult person to work with, in other ways I was a good person; I could motivate people.

I would think that even Mother Teresa in the early days got people to help, but in the way that she wanted. I don't want to make criticism of Mother Teresa, the outstanding person of our age, but I think it would be starry-eyed to think that the saints had all lovely qualities. Some had some very rough sides to them, particularly since I think that what really makes a saint is a total single-mindedness in doing what he perceives to be the will of God for him.

Going back to me, obviously there are many things in life I wish I hadn't done, though I don't believe in harking back to them; that wouldn't be a healthy thing to do. There are a number of cases where I've caused distress to somebody else, sometimes through no intention – just through bad luck really or just different cultures or not being alert enough to what they really wanted. I'm conscious of having upset people deeply when I never meant to and realising there was nothing I could do to put it right.

I know I'm impetuous. It's a strength and a weakness. And one's strength can be one's weakness. In the war, attacking a target, one of my strengths was that, the moment I saw half an opening, I would come in like a bolt and take them by surprise. I was quicker at assessing things in those days but I still tend to do that. Sometimes it's been very successful in finding a building for a Home, which, until fairly recently at any rate, had to be somewhere that didn't cost much money. In 1956 in Singapore my eye fell on an unused British Army jungle survival school. It was clearly ideal. When I asked the Commander-in-Chief if we could have it, he

looked me in the eyes and asked if I had the money to
run it if he gave it. At that stage, of course, we didn't,
but with the experience of starting ten Homes behind
me I knew we could get it and I answered: 'Yes'. In fact
I didn't have a dollar. And the Treasury in London
demanded the market price – thirty or forty thousand
pounds or more, completely out of the question. But
then the Singapore government took over and they
gave it to us for a dollar a year. So that was a case
where, if I hadn't decided quickly, it would have been
the end of it.

But there have been other occasions when I decided too quickly. I'm used to taking derelict structures
and building them up, but when you get a committee of
business people, their ways are completely different. In
Reno in the United States, I saw a building and wrote a
long memo giving all the reasons why I thought it was
ideal under the circumstances and they were obviously
completely right to reject it. It was a very cheap motel
built in a square; I thought it could have been made
more attractive, but it would not have been suitable for
disabled living and it would not have conformed to
modern standards. I would have done much better to
have left it entirely to their decision. For me to appear
out of the blue, spend an afternoon going round and
say, 'That's the building you should take,' wouldn't
carry much conviction with people who have lived
there all their lives and are men and women of some
standing. I'm slowly learning.

And I know I also have a tendency to want to hit
back. When the idea for my Memorial Fund came to
me, I saw the chance of a platform to launch it in a
prerecorded television interview for Remembrance Sunday with Harry Secombe.* I knew the ruling that you

can't appeal for money on television but I took a lot of trouble to find out from the programme makers if I could mention the Fund among other things. They said it was exactly what they wanted.

The night before, I went through agonies. I thought, 'Now look, if this is just a wishful idea of my own I will have gone public on something which is just a fancy thought, not something which has the hand of God behind it. On the other hand, if God is behind it, and I miss the opportunity, I've missed my chance. So what do I do?' Now I don't believe those sort of things are answered just by saying a prayer and getting an internal answer. So I thought, 'I know, I'll leave it in the hands of Harry Secombe and I'll say to him, "Are you absolutely sure that's what you want me to say?" And I made up my mind that, if I saw a flicker, or anything that made him pause, I would reject it. But there was no flicker. And when we came to sit down for the interview in the Cavendish Museum coffee room, he said, 'Well, Group Captain, you've got a new project, what is it?' After the interview he gave me £100 'for twenty of the lads'.

Then I got a letter from Anglia Television: 'Thank you so much for your most valuable contribution to the programme; you may notice that we have omitted all reference to an appeal.' My heart absolutely dropped. I'd missed my launch, and without the reference to the appeal, what I said would sound like nonsense. I was going to Parkminster for a day's retreat with the Carthusians and arrived there in a state of indignation. I thought it was very unjust and unprofessional. Dom Bruno said, 'You're being very stupid. God can give

* British television personality

you a much stronger platform than that any time he
wants, so just forget it.' Well my mind knew he was
right, but I could not get it out of my system. And in the
end I did, unfortunately, write a harsh letter to Anglia. I
prayed about it, I struggled with it, I said, 'No, I must
not write it.' But I still did.

*This business about hitting back though, I'm just won-
dering whether it's slightly at variance with your idea
of keeping your defences. All right, you wrote a tough
letter to Anglia, but if you had written a meek, polite
letter, they would probably think, 'Oh well, he doesn't
really mind,' and they'd go ahead and do the same
thing again to somebody else. Maybe it's sometimes
right to hit back.*

Yes, you're right. One must stand up against injustice and try to prevent it being repeated. In this case,
the cause of the Memorial Fund had definitely suffered.
But I also felt personally affronted, largely because we
had told everybody to watch the programme. I could
have written a completely different letter and made my
point just as forcefully but in a nice way. Anyway it's
made me make up my mind to try and be a bit more
reserved in future!

Yes I know we have to look after our own interests, but I'm trying to get it at the beginning of the
slippery slope. We have things that we set a lot of store
by but which are personal to us and I'm constantly
being caught out. I tend to react by immediately asking
myself how something affects me. On one occasion at
Dehra Dun, I was sitting there faced with a flat roof
which was going to collapse in the next monsoon and
with more mentally handicapped children and more

severely handicapped leprosy patients than I could possibly cope with, absorbed in all this, and wondering
where I could find help. This man came in, an Englishman, and his appearance wasn't particularly impres-
sive. From the way he said, 'Oh how pleased I am to
see you!' he gave me the impression he just wanted to
come in for a social chat. That was the one thing I
couldn't afford. I obviously invited him to come in, but
I was distant and wanted to get rid of him as soon as
possible. But he turned out to be the one man with a
solution to my problem, because he led me to an Oxfam
grant. My point is that I judged by appearances and I
can't have been watchful and looking at him in the right
way.

*But surely, ideally you should have had time for him
even if he wasn't bringing you some money! Maybe you
were particularly under stress at this time, but, it could
also be evidence that you're too wrapped up in your
work to have time for the little social things that maybe
aren't important to your work, but just make you human?*

I know I should have had time for him. But when
you're busy you've got to ration your time. Jesus didn't
have time for everybody. When somebody came to him
and said, 'Judge between me and my brother,' he said,
'Who appointed me to be judge over other people?' In
other words, that person was coming to him with a
request that was outside Jesus' terms of reference, so he
rejected them. When I was living in Dehra Dun where
there were 35 disabled people I made it a practice to
spend some time with each one everyday. There was
Mr Smith downstairs, an Anglo-Indian, who was very

lonely, so I would fight for five minutes with him. Now, if somebody's going to come and take half an hour of my time in the day just for social talk when I'm getting through my work, that's half an hour less that I've got to go round the Home, unless I'm going to cut into my sleep and I think that's a dangerous thing to start doing, unless there's a good reason for it. So it isn't that I don't spend time with people but the point is, with which people do you spend your time?

Now I'm quite certain I don't get it right and Gigi was saying only the other day, 'You don't seem to have the time now that you used to have for all sorts of different things.' Which I did. I spent a lot of time, as you say, doing the little social things. I think the reason is that, at this particular moment, I've got these two major jobs, the Homes which I can't default on and the Memorial Fund. I want to spend time with Jeromy and Gigi. I want urgently to spend time with Sue my wife, since our movements don't usually coincide. And yet I've got to get on with the duties that I've clearly got. Getting that balance right is very difficult. What I'm trying to say is that, in judging who you see and how much time you spend with them, shouldn't be judged by a calculation of self-interest.

I have to go to receptions and cocktail parties to meet supporters of a Home or to interest people in a new project but I don't find the setting easy. You never get down to any proper conversation with anybody. There's a high level of noise and you have to shout to make yourself heard. I haven't got the social graces. I'm not very good at talking until we're on a subject that I think is important, people are important but the subjects that are important to me are getting fewer and fewer. I've got a limited amount of thought time and

I'm finding more and more I just reject anything that's not within my terms of reference where I believe the work was given to me because there was no one else to take it on. I barely read the paper now. I find the effort of reading takes a lot of time and energy and I'd rather maximise my energies into fields where I think I can do something.

How do you cope with the volume of work?

My Father used to say: 'When you've got a pile of work you think you'll never get through, pick up each letter and do it as if it's the only letter you're going to do that day. Don't let your mind worry about the ones ahead.' Father Prior at Parkminster added, 'Yes, but don't let it escalate!' You can easily give a letter disproportionate time, which means you haven't got time left for the others beneath it. Once they get beyond a certain point, they depress me and I feel I'll never catch up. They keep coming in every day and I need to reduce them, otherwise they're a sort of hidden load on my mind and I keep thinking, 'That in-tray!' So I think you should discipline yourself to keep nibbling away at them.

Those letters sound as if they're the hardest aspect of your life!

Yes, I like to keep in touch with people who write to me; I like to write a personal answer, but at times it takes a huge amount of effort. There are very few letters I can just dash off. I find I've got to think how to compose them properly, but recently I've begun to worry less about style. I don't judge the time I give to

letters or people by their position in life, but by what
the content of the letter is. If I'm mentally tired, I pick
out the ones that don't need a lot of thought. Unless it's
a little boy or a student working on a thesis, I'm not
going to give as much time to a person who just writes
idly and says, 'Please send me a couple of pages on
your war experiences,' as I would to somebody who
says, 'My wife has died and I've got no purpose to my
life; can you suggest something?' One can fall back on
standard paragraphs to help out but I'm not as well-
organised on that as my wife is.

Have you ever felt things getting too much for you?

Well, just over a year ago, one day I felt very tired
and cancelled two engagements that day. I went to the
doctor and he said, 'You're overdoing it, you'll have to
take a month off and cut back what you're doing by 30
per cent. I'm not saying this lightly. If you don't do
what I tell you, something is going to happen.' He
could not have been more emphatic. So I came back
and said, 'OK I'll take a month off and try to cut back.'
Come September, a month later, this idea for my Memorial Fund suddenly came into my head. It came from
nowhere, but with a kind of inner compulsion and I
knew I had to react to it. From that moment on, I must
have added at least 30 per cent to what I was doing and
not only did I not take that month off but I haven't
taken a day off since then, except for my retreat, but
that's a different kind of time off. And I haven't been
back to that doctor since! I find if you get something
new to do, you're given an extra inner energy. That's
relevant to old people too, and I've seen it time and
time again in my life. It shows you can get introverted

and make your own judgements about what you can do and what you can't do, which is sometimes right and sometimes wrong.

But after the episode last year with the doctor, I also knew that I couldn't afford to carry anything that I didn't have to carry, not only non-essential work but also any inner load. For instance I thought, 'I cannot afford to carry a single niggle and if I get a brilliant idea for something I'm not going to entertain it, I'm just going to reject it all and give it to God – ask him straightaway to take it from me. Then I know if it's something he wants me to react to he'll give it back to me in the form that he wants.' It's the same thing with that niggle – once it's inside you, you can't cope with it, you wrestle and wrestle and wrestle and make all your good resolutions and pray but it's become part of you, so it's virtually impossible to discard. But if you meet it at the moment of impact, you can reject it, and that releases an enormous amount of energy. That worked very well for a year but recently I've slipped back a little. I must pull myself together.

The other thing, of course, is an awareness that, tomorrow, God may take me out of the running and put someone else in. He doesn't need me for the Memorial Fund. He has, I think, chosen me for the time being, but that may not necessarily be so tomorrow and if that's what he decides, well I accept it. But I still say, 'So long as I can run, I shall run.'

But do you ever relax?

Tennis is my main way of relaxing and trying to keep fit. But since the Memorial Fund, I've only played tennis every six weeks or so. I'm missing it badly, though I go and hit a ball against the wall two or three days a week. Taking the odd moment you can find, whether to run a couple of hundred yards, or get the feel of hitting the ball, I think is all-important. I've lost the ability to run a distance, but I can run for an hour and a quarter on the tennis court. It's different somehow – I'm chasing a tennis ball and I've got an opponent the other side whom I'm determined to knock down – if I can! My problem is how to find the time not to let my tennis slip away altogether. I believe in doing any little thing you can. Whether it's overcoming a little fault or just some indoor exercises, take every opportunity to get back to it. Once you form a good habit, it becomes easy.

I gave up cigarettes in 1948 because I realised they'd got a hold on me; I was their slave and I resented it. I gave up initially for two years after a huge struggle and then smoked one cigarette and was back where I started. Then I gave them up again at the time when I was becoming a Catholic. Fr Clarke was just no help at all. He said, 'Come on now, you know you're not going to keep this up, so have this cigarette!' No, I never told my children not to smoke. I don't see that it's immoral. Gigi doesn't smoke at all and Jeromy does. I always enjoyed a drink, and never thought I'd be able to give that up, but the day came when it just made me feel muzzy, so it's got no appeal to me now.

I used to like listening to music at odd moments. I used to enjoy television programmes like Dad's Army – we watched it as a family – and Starsky and Hutch, but I don't really any more. Though I have got unbounded admiration for Fred Astaire and, occasionally, if I feel I need a break, I might look at a Fred Astaire film. I remember Jeromy saying to me one day, 'Oh Dad, I think you ought to spoil yourself sometimes!' – I was rather touched! But ever since the Memorial Fund, life has just become too full. It's not that I wouldn't enjoy the programme, just that my mind's not on it.

No, I don't take a holiday. I did when Jeromy and Gigi were young. We all four went together. I don't even think I have a day off. I make a rule not to do my letters on a Sunday, but I do other things. I'll read or do work that isn't strictly business. I do want to keep it a special day. I think that is something we Christians need to examine our consciences on. If we don't observe Sunday in a way that we're claiming it should be observed, then we can't really expect the government to support us on, say, limiting Sunday shopping.

But I also think it's a good thing to get away from your work. I can get so tired sometimes that I just sit at a letter and look at it and can't compose an answer, but if I come back to it the next morning I'll suddenly manage a run of twenty letters.

As for sleep, I need at least six hours and prefer seven. I've often tried to get up early, but I'm definitely not at my best and find that I wilt during the day. My wife gets up very early and I usually just let her get up and go off to sleep again. I find it an awful effort getting up in the morning.

And what sort of things irritate you?

All sorts of little things – I mean funny little things like somebody shuffling and rustling through papers. It gets on my nerves. Noise that has a purpose I don't mind, someone drilling the road, but purposeless noise, or what I feel is purposeless, I do. Some voices grate on me; if people are too pushy and pleased with

themselves, it puts me off. You have to learn to overcome those feelings because, I mean, we do the same to
other people and people are pretty forbearing and understanding with me, so I ought to be the same with
them. But public confessions are not really very nice
things are they?

Would you recommend your lifestyle to others?

I certainly wouldn't – unless it was their natural
life. Artificially to put themselves into another person's
position would not be right. I don't see that you can
compare one life with another or one job with another
and say, 'This is a better job than that.' The question is,
which is right for you. People come along and say, 'I
wish I was doing some good like you are doing'. Well I
do understand the thought behind the question but on
the other hand I don't really agree with it because every
job that's well done is contributing to a better world. If
there weren't people who designed and ran airlines, I
wouldn't be able to go about my job. You couldn't have
everybody going around looking after the disabled and
lonely, could you? You'll still have opportunities to do
things for other people in a voluntary way. I think that
what matters is that we recognise the need to devote
part of our time to advancing the good of others and to
advance the interests of others in advancing your own.
You can't possibly lay down a rule as to what people
should do. It's very personal. But you do also need to
remember not to neglect the family you brought about,
or they won't be going out into the world fully equipped.
Small things are so important. When the British
Army was retreating at Dunkirk and being bombed
without any anti-aircraft protection on an open beach, a

little company of Guards arrived and saw that there was near-panic, so the Sergeant-Major lined them up as if they were on the parade ground and made them drill. Now you could well say, 'What a ridiculous thing to do!' But the effect on the beach was electrifying, because when the others saw this going on, they pulled themselves together and remembered their training and their duty and forgot their panic. So the lesson is that one man setting a little example against the tide that's flowing in the wrong direction can change it. But we tend to think that, unless we do something spectacular, it's no good. I can't accept that there's ever nothing you can do, whatever your circumstances. Unemployed people should be encouraged to take up some hobby; helping people or study or something which they find inwardly rewarding, instead of staying at home and drinking beer and thinking, 'What will I do, I haven't got a job?' A disabled person, who can't take a job, frequently puts his life to good use.

10
Journey's end

'I pray that you'll have a long life but a good life.'
Mother Teresa to Cheshire

You said to me quite early on, that one of the major themes in your thinking is that God has a purpose for all. How have you been so convinced of that?

I had a rather unusual experience, though I've since discovered that something like it has happened to others. I was seeing Jeromy off at St Pancras station. I turned to walk away but then I decided I would just stand and wait until the train was out of sight. And as I did so, in an instant, everything completely changed. Even the sound of the engine was totally different; it was a sort of deep throb that seemed to enter the whole of my being, like the roar of many, many waters. Suddenly, too, every single thing and movement had a meaning to it. Everybody was walking about, or picking up, carrying or putting down their bags – somehow I seemed able to see inside the train itself. They were all going in different directions, but everything that they were doing was co-ordinated and deeply, profoundly purposeful. The train was taking them off to some unknown place to accomplish something of great importance in which they all had a crucial role to play. And added to that, there was a most extraordinary feeling of authority. It's actually impossible to describe; it overwhelmed me. You're used to people doing things under authority, but never remotely to this degree and in this way. There was authority, purpose and power, immense power, all three mysteriously interrelated and giving added meaning and depth to each other. Then suddenly it all disappeared and we were back to normal. That was three years or so ago and at intervals I have quietly pondered it, for at the time I didn't really know what message it had, except that it reinforced my conviction that we are here on earth for a deep purpose whose fulfilment we will only see in the next world.

Every single act that we do is invested with a deep purpose, if only we could see it. If you look at the universe, you've got the outer stars, the constellations, shooting away from us at several times the speed of light; every atom of space that fills the cosmos is bounding with energy. Then if you come back and look at the inherent power in the smallest atom, or the beauty and complexity of a little snowflake, you see the immense variety and at the same time the unity of created matter. Now God is outside it – you can't picture where, or rather what that means – yet he's present in every single part, holding it in existence. If he took his hand away, it would all drop like a book drops from my hand if I let it go, but he's not only holding it in existence, he's guiding it towards the end he has in mind. We discover that plan largely by the things that happen to us, by praying for guidance and then by the correct use of our reason. When Arthur suddenly appeared in front of me, I wasn't thinking of God's plan but he clearly led me into what he had in mind for me.

Jesus' life was nothing but contradiction and suffering from start to finish. Born in a stable, hounded by the authorities wherever he went, betrayed by his closest friends, abandoned by his disciples, he was condemned to the most shameful and agonizing death possible, yet nothing diverted him from fulfilling the plan his Father had for him. Not a single harsh feeling for those who were doing him to death, instead, 'Father forgive them for they know not what they do.' He had all these totally unjust and terrible set-backs and sheer suffering inflicted on him, but in each case he was able to bring good out of it.

We may well think, 'Why does God ask me to do this and then block me,' but the question is, are we going to be influenced by what we see as a set-back, or are we going to keep our eyes focused on God and know that, if it's happened, it must be for the best? If we could only hold onto the knowledge that, no matter what dreadful disaster or suffering has seized us, God is right in the middle of it!

The trouble is, we only see things from a limited point of view. Let me go back to the war. In 1941 the Allied campaign in Greece and Crete was seen by most people as absolutely hopeless. The Germans managed to land and either killed or captured all the Allied troops there. But there's no doubt at all that the Greek and Cretan campaign was a major contributing factor in forcing Hitler to delay his attack on Russia. And remember that, just as he got to the outskirts of Moscow, winter came down and halted him. Had he reached Moscow earlier, he would have occupied it and no one can tell what would then have happened to the war. So what appeared to be a totally futile campaign in fact contributed in a major way to final victory.

Take my first venture with the ex-servicemen, which failed totally. It just left me with nothing, an impossible load of debts, everybody gone, nobody to advise me, unable to see the future. I was young and it didn't discourage me, but it appeared to be a total failure and when the BBC, years later, made the first film on the Homes, they called it 'Founded on Failure' – quite a nice title!

If something is worthwhile, it's going to have many set-backs at the beginning. I had that feeling with my Memorial Fund. I was convinced I would get several millions from the Berlin rock concert, 'The Wall'*

* On 21 July 1990

– but I was wrong. I had no idea how disorganised some elements of the rock world are! But in a way it was a blessing because I felt I had been getting over-confident. Yet it did get me established in countries like the USA and Germany where we'd been making no headway. And I was greatly moved by that sea of calm but intense young faces and the warmth when some of them spotted me and came to talk to me about the Fund afterwards. I've always found that, if there are set-backs, you mustn't be upset, you should really be pleased. Because if you accept the set-back without losing faith in the project, you're expressing more faith in God. Mother Teresa says, 'Whatever God gives, take, and whatever God takes, give, and with a smile – no, two smiles.'

The difficulties when you're on the right path are ones you can see have got to be overcome, but those that beset you when you're on the wrong road, or when you exceed your authority, are different. In a funny way that I can't describe, nothing quite fits – and that's a warning sign. It's the sentry again, challenging every thought that comes to you, 'Friend or foe?'

You constantly stress that you've got a long way to go before you're perfect – nevertheless, you do appear to be thinking a lot more about your faith – and probably praying a lot more – than the average person. Some people, even Christians, might find your dedication rather awesome. Did you never have a crisis of faith after your conversion? Or took any steps backwards, or had any regrets?

No, a crisis of faith, never. Steps backwards, that's something different. There must have been many, of many different kinds, and in prayer too. There was a time in the beginning, the first five, six, seven years, when I probably prayed over-intensely and then gradually settled down. Then there came a period of nearly ten years when I just left it as it was, sort of freewheeled. We do that, don't we? Go in fits and starts! But I feel that was a great loss. Fortunately in the spiritual life nothing is ever too late and it seems to me important to take things in a relaxed way.

You seem to rely greatly on the Church's teaching. Have you never had any doubts about it?

I know that individuals will never be completely right. Even the great Christian intellectuals. And even if they are right in nearly everything they say, they probably haven't got the relationship of all the different elements of the faith right. Even Thomas Aquinas* went wrong on one or two points. That's why we need a guaranteed teaching authority and that's why I'm suspicious of arguments that sound very plausible aimed at countermanding something that's been traditional in the Church's teaching. It's a good thing that people should enquire, but if you're going to set the appeal of the argument against the authority being exerted from the teaching Church, then I think you're probably misguided.

However I think, in the last resort, we are responsible for our own moral judgements. The Church will issue principles; we have to apply them. We can't shed

* Italian Dominican saint and theologian (1224-74). His *Summa Theologiae* and *Summa Contra Gentiles* form the classical systematization of Roman Catholic theology

our own moral responsibility by saying, 'The Church has told me this and therefore it's right, so I'll do it,' because every individual situation is different, and so God has given us a conscience as well as a teaching authority. There's the just rule of law in society, but there's also an inner law written on the heart of man, in the inner sanctuary of our being. Now we have a duty to develop the sensitivity, the openness of our conscience to the promptings of the Holy Spirit and we do that partly by listening to what the Church has to say, partly by discussing it with people who are competent to make a judgement, but above all by responding to our conscience. I think I'd say that, where there is an honest and upright search for the truth and a genuine willingness to live by what your conscience tells you, then there is morality. The danger is that we think in terms of absolutes. Jesus says, 'Be perfect as my father in heaven is perfect,' and we say, 'Well how can I be perfect?' (Matthew 5:45-48). That isn't the point. He's really asking us here and now this minute to be doing our best. That's why the little things are important. So it's an evolving process and you can never say you've achieved it. The point is to keep on the road.

But as someone who's liked going his own way – and especially as you talk about following your conscience – I wonder if there have been elements of the Church's teaching which you've been unhappy with? The question of artificial birth control is always brought up, but you've worked a lot in India and other parts of the Third World where it's become a particularly thorny issue, linked with aid programmes for example and almost everyone except the Catholic Church holding out for it...

If the human family was created by God for a specific purpose, then it follows that he must have built into it a series of laws which enable us to conduct our relations in harmony and achieve life's objective. If I want to learn to fly it would be nonsense if somebody says to me, 'Don't be stupid, why should somebody tell you what to do in the air.' In order to gain the freedom of the skies, you've got to learn and obey the laws of flight. So to me the law that is a true law, that's issued with authority and knowledge, far from being restrictive, is actually giving me freedom. So the laws of the Church I don't find difficult to accept at all, so long as I know they are the laws of the Church. Most people say to me, 'You're the fellow who always likes to go his own way; how can you submit to the authority of Rome?' But the Christian laws are not so much laws, they are an expression of love. Because God wants the best for us in order to help us achieve our end, he's given us, as it were, signposts. Laws can be defined as signposts along the road to eternal life.

But I have to try and be very honest here and admit that there are controversial aspects of the Church's teaching on morals that I haven't really addressed my mind to as I should. Now, can I state my basic position again? Whatever the Church teaches as part of the fundamentals of Christian faith or morals and teaches unswervingly, I accept.

The argument is not about birth control – the Church has always insisted on the need for what it calls responsible parenthood – it's about the method of birth control. The Church's claim is that there is a natural family planning method and, if properly understood and used, it is highly effective; but I acknowledge that it presents a few difficulties. In the first place, I have got a faint feeling that the Church may not have said the last word on it. In the second place, I don't feel completely comfortable in defending natural family planning against the person who seems utterly convinced that it isn't realistic and that over-population is a major cause of the world's problems. But the issue is a lot more complex than it looks at first sight. I'm not convinced that the world is really incapable of feeding and giving adequate living standards to the population as it is calculated to become in a hundred years' time.

I'm not trying to express a thought-out viewpoint, I'm trying to say that there are arguments on both sides. And when I hear somebody from a family of five saying that people should only have two children, I wonder which of them they think shouldn't have been born. Looking at it impersonally and numerically is one thing, looking at it in terms of actual people, face to face, is another. Are we in danger of saying, 'Well I'm on earth, and why should there be too many people causing me a problem?' Until I'm totally convinced that artificial birth control is consistent with the teachings of Christ, then I'm against it.

You're obviously very keen to tell people about your faith – but do you think there's any way of persuading someone actually to believe in God?

No. I'm doubtful that you can prove logically that the God whom Christianity proclaims as God really does exist. You meet people who want to believe and are searching and they take different stances, but trying to convince them in my experience doesn't get very far – though perhaps it does in an unseen way that bears fruit later. I've often discussed this with David Lean. I was very fond of him; he was one of the few friends I occasionally went out and relaxed with. He would say that it was mad 'to think that the Rolls Royce standing by the side of the road had come into being by accident; there had to be a first cause.' Therefore there had to be a first cause for creation, but what it was he had no idea. Perhaps a great charge of electricity? Well, I said, 'That doesn't carry much conviction because a charge of electricity can't be responsible for the nobility and beauty of spirit that is in man.' Then, a year or two later, David said, 'I agree there must be a creator who created the universe, but I feel he's left it to run on its own, like a man who paints a beautiful painting or produces a great film and then goes off and leaves it.' My answer to that was, 'But David, that painting and that film only continue to exist because there are living men to take care of them, to maintain the environment at the right temperature and humidity and so on, so that argument strengthens my case, not yours.' He reflected for a while and then came back to what I think was his main obstacle: 'I look at the suffering in the world and at the things the Church has done and I can't reconcile it with your belief. I wish I knew the answer.'

You've also frequently mentioned Satan as a factor in your thinking – and in the early days of your conversion, the 'Screwtape Letters' which sees Satan very much as a person was a strong influence on you. But do you actually believe that Satan is at work in the world in the traditional sense – of an actual malignant force?

I can't prove that Satan exists but I know perfectly well that he does, and, from experience, I know some of the ways in which he operates. In the early days of my work with the Homes, I sat by many deathbeds. One stands out in my mind. The person in question had only been with us for a short time and then was taken ill and lay dying, so I knew nothing about her background. There is usually a dignity in dying, but, in this case, I felt something completely different. There wasn't any conversation, because she'd gone into a coma, but I had a very uncomfortable feeling that something was wrong, a very strong feeling of the presence of evil, not in her, I don't think, but all around her. It had such an effect on me that I was quite afraid. I lived alone at the time in a little, fairly isolated cottage and I had to walk back to it. I felt very uncomfortable at doing that. Now, that's a subjective experience and it may just have been imagination, but it was very strong. I can even half still feel it today.

Satan's strength lies in his ability to disguise himself in a thousand and one different ways, almost always under the appearance of something that's good. If Hitler hadn't presented some good arguments, the nation wouldn't have followed him. And linked with that is this use of sanitised language. Abortion is described as 'terminating a pregnancy', whereas the truth is, it's terminating a life. The supporters of nuclear deterrence, myself included, used to refer to nuclear targets as confined to 'key elements of state power'. Like 'terminating a pregnancy', that sounds reassuring but whatever form that 'key element' takes, it's virtually bound to be close to a built-up area.

Satan can stir up your emotions. When you're slightly angry he can make you angrier. Perhaps you're about to do something quite good and he'll suddenly make you think, 'I'm a bit hungry and I'll have some lunch first'. Sometimes he'll make a direct assault on you and try and push you into something.

But Satan won't succeed directly in persuading people that there's no God. What he will do is mis-represent God, as he did with Eve, and twist God so he takes on a different appearance in our minds, like a dreadful taskmaster. And he's influenced man into be-coming the sole determiner of what is right and what is wrong. And that lies at the root of everything that's gone wrong.

For example, people object strongly to the sug-gestion that, say, free sex is immoral. They say, 'Who are you to say it's immoral,' so society wants to be its own arbiter.

So what would you suggest as a solution?

Once you recognise what's happening, turn im-mediately to God and ask his help. Satan will then drop that tactic because it's counter-productive. On our own, there's no hope whatsoever of seeing through Satan's ruses, or getting the better of him. But although Satan is so powerful and intelligent, the whole world of grace is complete darkness to him. He can't see his way through it because he's cut himself off from God. He's got love for himself but hatred for everything else. So one comfort is that he and the devils can't be a co-ordinated body, so they must be fighting against each other. And at the same time, he can have no power over us unless we actually co-operate, so we can't use Satan as an excuse for whatever harm we've done. The more we become his agents, the more he has power in the world.

On the other hand, might you be in danger of sounding anachronistic? After all, the word 'Satan', used so bluntly, doesn't crop up a lot nowadays. Perhaps many

people would say he doesn't really exist quite in that
way. And even 'Sin' tends not to be used so much.

I'm convinced it's part of Satan's reasoning,
making it unfashionable to talk about himself. I went to
a talk that Hans Küng gave. I must say much of it was
inspiring but much didn't appeal to me at all. I don't
mean Hans Küng as a person, but because everything
he presented was done in a way which boosted himself
at the expense of somebody else. He made fun of the
Pope, he made fun of the Vatican, but he did it in such a
way that, very subtly, he seemed to me to be lifting
himself up. And there's a very basic principle that the
prophet must not profit, so that put me off. Then somebody mentioned Satan and in a very angry way, he
lifted his finger and said, 'No!' But Jesus constantly
talks about Satan in many different contexts.

And I argue that it's another of the devil's tri-
umphs that he's made the mention of sin something to
be rather shied away from, not quite proper to talk
about it in ordinary conversation. But the more you
lose your sense of sin, the more you lose your sense of
God and conversely, the more you approach God, the
more you're aware of the reality and horror of sin. If
we're sorry, God will forgive us and the guilt is forgotten. But every sin has its consequence; no matter how
sorry we are, the damage that's done remains. I'll give
you an example. At one o'clock in the morning one
Easter Monday night, fire broke out at one of our Homes.
It turned out later that it was arson. Well, all the residents were evacuated but one of them died the next day
because of smoke inhalation. Now just suppose the
culprit was me and suppose that I come to regret what
I've done deeply. I go along and genuinely ask to be

forgiven with all my heart. I am forgiven. But that forgiveness doesn't bring back the person who died and restore her to her husband, nor does it put right the traumatic effect of that fire on all the residents of that Home. And in that Home they had lived together as a family; now they suddenly had to be separated and they didn't know what their future was. Picture the state of mind that they were in. My point is, you have to do something to help repair the damage you have caused.

Now, when we come to look at the final judgement, that awesome moment when God will judge the entire world, and each of us individually, according to what we've done, and will require us to give an account of ourselves, I think we need to understand that we'll all face the people whom we've harmed and the people whom we've done good to. In the here and now, we make the best judgements we can about ourselves and our actions and so on. For instance I have made a judgement that the bomber offensive was justified, but I realise perfectly well that, when it comes to the end of time, and I have to stand before God and give an account of my actions, I'll be confronted with the people whom my bombs killed, and that God will be the judge. And it will be the same with every single lobby, every single group who worked or fought for a common objective and every single individual. The person who upholds abortion or takes any part in it will be faced with that helpless infant whose life he or she terminated, the anti-abortionists with the mothers who thought that they lost their freedom, and God will judge.

As you get older, moving through your seventies, do you find yourself thinking of your own death? Or just of old age?

Well, I think of old age in the sense that I realise how much still remains to be done and that if I'm going to give of my best, which, please God, I will, I've got to have more back up. One thing I'm absolutely certain – as you get older – that you need to keep yourself fully stretched and occupied. The minute you say, 'Well I can afford to give it up, I'll just sit around for a while and read the papers and more or less freewheel', you're on the way to fading gradually away.

Death? Well that's a bigger subject. Perhaps I should think about it consciously more. What I find, but I have to pay heed to what Dom Bruno says on this point, is that when I think or try to think of heaven, my immediate thought is that I've got to do better with what remains of my life on earth. I find that I simply can't just start thinking how wonderful life there will be. I'm here on earth, as it were in the middle of the battleground, people are suffering, people have doubts, people have difficulties, they're struggling in all sorts of ways. I don't want to leave that for my own good. I know perfectly well, as Dom Bruno points out, that it isn't because of our own merits that we're going to share God's life. I realise that, by trying to live a good life, we are all going to be rewarded in heaven. Once again we're faced with a paradox. Heaven is a pure gift of God. At the same time, the faith too is a gift and since I've been given it, I've got responsibilities here on earth. Then I long for other people also to get the gift of the faith, so I'm torn in two directions.

Death is something that you must have encountered frequently – but the first time, with Arthur Dykes must have been difficult – what did you learn from it?

The hospital had impressed on me that I mustn't tell Arthur he was dying. Arthur had said to me, 'Len, just give me a little piece of land at Le Court and I'll get myself a caravan and live there and organise myself.' And I thought, I can't let this man make plans for the future when he's got no hope whatsoever of realising them, so I came to the conclusion that I had to tell him he was dying. And I braced myself and went in and said, 'Arthur, I'm very sorry to say this, but I don't think you're going to recover,' and he looked at me and sort of gave a sigh and fell back on his pillows and said, 'Thank God I know.' He'd been agonising you see. So I learnt then that, whilst you can't generalise, there are a great many people who'd prefer to know rather than not know. The only thing is, I think you must approach the subject very gently at the right moment and watch the person – do they want to take it a step further or do they want to shy off?

One evening, about eight o'clock, I realised that Arthur was going to die. I'd seen people killed in aircraft crashes and I'd seen dead bodies, but I'd never actually been face to face with a man who was in the course of dying. That was quite a big experience which I had to adjust to. So I rang the hospital and said, 'What am I going to do?' and they said, 'It's perfectly simple: just wait until you think he's dead, then wait another three hours and if you're still convinced he's dead, lay him out.' 'What does that mean?' I said. 'Well you wash him and put a pair of clean pyjamas on him, and in the morning ring up the doctor.' So I said 'Ok', and I sat by him and didn't quite know what to say or do. I was saying stupid things like, 'Would you like a cigarette?' and I could see him look at me and then look away.

   With other people, in the early days of the Homes, I thought, 'I've got to say something very edifying,' but that was rather artificial and I didn't know what to say. I quite soon discovered that that was completely wrong and what I needed to do was just to give such human company and support as I could. I was told, and I'm convinced it's true, that the last of the senses to go is that of hearing and that, even though a dying person is unconscious, in a coma and unable to respond to anything, he can still hear what you're saying. In fact, I believe that what you say resounds through his head so that the first essential thing is that you must never say anything about that person to a third party that you wouldn't want him to hear. The second thing is that you should be reassuring and comforting. It's all very well for people to say, 'Well I'm passing into the hands of God,' but we don't know what's going to happen between the moment that death approaches and the final outcome. We can be pretty certain that it's going to be a lonely journey and there's bound to be a sadness — because you're leaving all the people that you love — and this world that was given to us to make good use of. So that person does need company and support, just being there and holding his hand and just saying a nice little something to him. And I think I can say that nearly every death I've seen has been edifying. First, to see the extraordinary capacity to hang onto life, long after the doctors think that the person's going to die. They seem to go on, sometimes two or three days longer and then there always seems to me a dignity in that dying.

But are you at all afraid of dying? Or perhaps do you wish death would hurry along a bit — being a man with great faith, that would be logical wouldn't it?

I don't think I'm afraid. Though I realise that, having been involved in so much destruction and killing in the war, if I had to, well, die a fairly violent death, I could hardly complain. I know that I did what I saw was necessary, but nevertheless I've been close to a great deal of other people's suffering and I have been relatively untouched myself. Fair is fair.

One side of me may want death to come soon, but person after person has been saying to me over the past years and in fact it has touched me deeply 'May God give you many more years to go on working.' Once you're dead, the chance is gone. I don't believe that, when you die, you lose your involvement in this world. I'm totally at one with St Therese of Lisieux when she said, 'I want to spend my heaven doing good on earth,' and if I were asked my greatest wish, I think it would probably be that. But of course your involvement is of a completely different order. I mean here we are, as I say, on the battlefield and I would rather stay on the battlefield as long as I can in the hope that I can be a good combatant.

Our dying is really the most important part of our lives. The here and now and one's death are part and parcel of the same thread. I mean your dying actually starts at the moment of your birth because you're moving towards the moment when you die. But God is going to give me the chance of completing my task right up to the very end, even if I've left it to the last minute, like the labourers in the vineyard.

I've got a story that may illustrate that – about Sir Douglas Bader* and Bomber Harris.** I've got to

* See chapter 6
** Sir Arthur Harris, Commander-in-Chief of RAF Bomber Command 1942-45

preface it by telling you that both Dougie and Bomber
Harris were very strong characters. They expressed
themselves very forcefully; each had a very pungent
sense of humour and a certain aggressiveness in a nice
way. Dougie Bader, who wasn't a religious man by any
means, had, over many years, been saying to me, 'Len,
come along and spend a night with us and let's have a
good long talk. Don't leave it too long, or it may be too
late.' Well he lived down at Newbury and I can't say it
was very convenient for me, but I kept saying, 'Oh one
day,' but sadly, I never got there.

Now, this particular night, there was a big Bomber
Command reunion. I walked up the steps and as I got
into the entrance hall, there, sitting on the right, was
Dougie Bader. He immediately called out, 'Come here,
boy and sit beside me!' Now there was something
about the way he said it that was different. I got the
feeling he really wanted to have a talk. As I mentioned
in that incident with the fire in New Zealand, one
notices in life that there are times that people say something in such a way that you feel there's a particular
meaning in it. I went and sat next to Dougie, but of
course everybody wanted to crowd round him, so there
was no opportunity for talking. Then he had to give an
after dinner speech and so did Bomber Harris. When
Dougie got up to speak, I was immediately struck by
the fact that there was something different about him, a
sort of gentle quality, not actually self-deprecating, but
a kind of humbleness that must have been in his character, but didn't so obviously come through and it made
a very deep impression on me. After he sat down,
Bomber Harris got up, and I had exactly the same
feeling that, suddenly, there was a new gentleness and
there was something different about him. He said things

that I'd never heard him say before, for instance, 'The man up there may be thinking...', and he looked and pointed upwards. He was now ninety or so, though I don't think his mind was wandering, but it gave me a feeling that something had changed. Neither of them had any faith, but both seemed to me to be taking the first, faltering steps. That's the point.

In the morning when I woke up at eight o'clock, I turned the radio on and the first words that the announcer said were, 'Group Captain Sir Douglas Bader,' so I knew that could only mean that he'd died. He'd died in the car on the way home. And, as it happened, that was also the last after dinner speech that Bomber Harris ever made. I suppose there's no real justification for drawing a conclusion, but I have always felt that the change in each of their attitudes was somehow related to their approaching deaths.

Death is the moment when we are standing at the gates of heaven. We are half way between this life and what we call eternity, and our future capacity to fulfil our role in eternity is going to be governed to a large extent by the way we accept our death. I simply do not believe we can be sure that dying is going to be easy. I'm on uncertain ground here, but when Arthur was dying he seemed to be going through a struggle. He'd suddenly look up and say, 'Yes I suppose I've got to go.' There was something going on there, some deep inner – not only questioning, but I think wrestling, in which I had no part. When from time to time I said something, he just looked at me without comprehending – it was as though it was just a diversion. I am convinced there is a final battle, a profound, inner battle that nobody outside can see, the Devil on his side making his last assault on us and God on his side doing everything in his power to appeal to us. It may well be that God may appear remote. He did to Jesus on the Cross: 'My God, my God, why have you forsaken me!' That cry affects me deeply. I'm convinced that, in our dying, we have to share something of Christ's death. We can't expect death just to be a simple passing over. And a nurse told me the story of a dying man in a deep sleep. When in the morning he woke up, she said to him, 'Mr Smith, how peaceful you looked, I've never seen anybody look so peaceful.' He answered, 'Peaceful! All night there's been a horrible figure banging on the window trying to get in and I spent the whole time shouting, 'You have no right to come in, you have no right to come in, I refuse to let you in!' No, beneath that very peaceful exterior there was going on a deep inner battle, and his will was made up; he was not going to let that figure in.

Last year's Festival of Remembrance in the Albert Hall in London suddenly seemed to have a little message for me about our death. In the centre is the large arena on which the action takes place, and round it, tier upon tier of spectators, a cross-section of the nation with the Queen at their head. The action mostly consists of displays by the armed forces, but others enter the stage too – somebody who was wounded in the war, some ex-nursing auxiliaries, a land army girl, a widow and so on. They are first announced, then enter via a short tunnel and down some steps and everybody's straining to see them, clapping and cheering as they walk across the arena. Well, in a tiny way, I think that's a mirror of the day we enter heaven. The moment of our dying is an extremely solemn moment, it's a moment of the most profound possible meaning, not just to us but to the myriads and myriads who already inhabit Heaven, who see it as a marvellous victory – of Christ who made it possible, but also of us who, too, paid a price. You could even say there's a third victory, of all those who've helped us on our way. Each person who enters heaven adds to the joy of everybody else there. So different from our attitude on earth!

And do you think there's a hell?

I think hell is something many of us wish wasn't part of the Christian Faith, but it only requires a little objective thought to realise that if it weren't, something would be wrong with the Church's teaching about heaven. What the Church is telling us is that hell is a real possibility, a possibility that you cannot deny unless you deny that God has created us free to make up our own minds about him. Therefore the Church is absolutely right in preaching about hell and doing what it can to make us take it seriously. After all if, despite everything that God has done for me and despite his last approaches to me at the hour of my death, I remain completely and finally obdurate in refusing him, well then, he has to respect my free and deliberate choice. It will then be I, not he, who excludes myself from his presence.

But it is utterly beyond us even to begin to imagine the lengths to which he is prepared to go to prevent that. Only when we come to see this at the awesome moment of the final judgement, will we understand the mystery of suffering. Then we will know the answer to that soldier's cry on the battlefield of the Somme, 'Where's God in all this?'

Appendix

Leonard Cheshire Foundation
26 Maunsel Street
London SW1P 2QN

Charity No: 218186

Has 270 Homes in 49 countries providing residential care for disabled people, mostly younger adults. Some Homes specialize in mental handicap, others in the mentally ill. Family Support Services offer part-time care to disabled people living in their own homes.

Sue Ryder Foundation
Cavendish
Suffolk CO10 8AY

Charity No: 222291

Founded by Sue Ryder (now Baroness Ryder of Warsaw) as a living memorial to those killed in war or by persecution. Just over 80 homes in 14 countries for the disabled and sick of all ages. Also operates Domiciliary Services.

Ryder-Cheshire Mission
for the relief of suffering
Staunton Harold Hall
Ashby de la Zouche
Leicestershire LE4 5RT

Charity No: 285746

Founded by Leonard Cheshire and his wife, Baroness Ryder of Warsaw, in 1959. It undertakes projects outside the scope of the Leonard Cheshire and Sue Ryder Foundations, but for which there is a clear need, mostly in the developing countries.

The Memorial Fund
for Disaster Relief
3 Throgmorton Avenue
London EC2N 2WW

Charity No: 803119

Aims to collect £5 (US$10) for each of the 100 million lives lost in the wars of this century to create a global fund, the interest of which will go to disaster relief. 'Remember a life to save a life.'

FAMILY OF PRAYER
for disabled people and their helpers
'could you not watch with me one hour?'

RAPHAEL PILGRIMAGE
Every September to Lourdes with 70 severely disabled pilgrims.

Enquiries for the above to Ryder-Cheshire Mission.